ON BEING
A GAY PARENT

ON BEING
A GAY PARENT

Making a Future Together

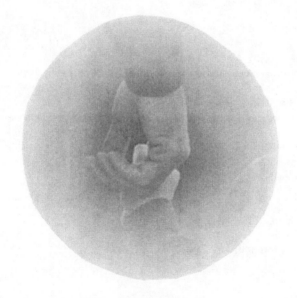

by Brett Webb-Mitchell

Seabury Books
an imprint of Church Publishing Incorporated
New York

Cover design by Corey Kent

Interior design by Carol Sawyer

Webb-Mitchell, Brett.
 On being a gay parent : making a future together / by Brett Webb-Mitchell.
   p. cm.
 ISBN 978-1-59627-061-9 (pbk.)
 1. Parenting—Religious aspects—Christianity. 2. Gay parents. 3. Family—Religious life.
 I. Title.

BV4529.W435 2007
248.8'4508664—dc22
                    2007030567

Church Publishing, Incorporated.
445 Fifth Avenue
New York, New York 10016

5 4 3 2 1

To Adrianne and Parker,
a.k.a., the Divine Miss A and Parker Parker
who made it possible for me to write this book;

∾

To Dean, who has taken the role as the
"gay nanny" in stride;

∾

To the countless women and men
who, as lesbians and gays,
are enjoying the happiness and
challenges of being parents in this age of conflict.

∾

Contents

Introduction

NAVIGATING THE
SPEED BUMPS

It is not so much that things happen in a family as it
is that the family *is* the things that happen in it.

—FREDERICK BUECHNER[1]

This is *not* the book on families that I intended to write several
years ago. Not only has my definition or description of what a
modern American family looks like changed, but the composition of *my* family has changed.

About a decade ago, I was under contract to write an academic
textbook on the changing patterns of being a family in modern
American society in relationship to the changing Church. From
the onset, I had firm convictions about the changing nature of
the family, and so the task seemed to be simple and straight-
forward. The book was to be based on the readings and work I
had done with families for a long time. As an undergraduate,
I spent a great deal of time with children with disabilities and
their families. I took family therapy courses in seminary; I took
part in family therapy as a client; I served as a pastoral counselor

in churches; and I worked as a pseudo-family therapist in a supervised setting when I was the Director of Religious Life at Devereux Center for young people with emotional, behavioral, and developmental disabilities.

The previous book's chapter structure was based on the outline of a course that I was teaching when I was an assistant professor of Christian nurture at Duke Divinity School. *That* book is not *this* book. When I was teaching the course and preparing to write about families, I was a "happy" and successful member of the faculty of a large and prestigious divinity school; I was happily married, with two small, charming, healthy, bright children; we owned our home; we vacationed with the extended family in Oregon. We had two cars, one cat, and were contemplating a dog as our next pet. We lived in the privileged, wealthy, academic community of Chapel Hill–Carrboro, North Carolina. Everything was good. We were an up-and-coming family. We were a dazzling example of the all-American family! Long live the family!

But, underneath it all, as is true for so many families around the world, there were seeds of discontent that would soon sprout, grow, and change the course of our family's life. While some who are mortgaged to and thus beholden to the American dream but who are living a life similar to what was my own are still there, others, like myself, have found that living more truthful, wholesome, and healthier lives is not only the better option, but the only option.

Like so many, I knew I was gay at an early age. Or, to be more exact, I was around eleven or twelve years old, literally stuck in the closet with my best friend during a routine afternoon game of cops and robbers. We were the robbers, in hiding. I was with my best friend, and I didn't want anyone to find us in the closet. I was happy being silent with my best friend, our bodies pressed against each other, his hand over my mouth as I wanted to laugh and scream in delight over these otherwise pretend circumstances.

Throughout junior high school and high school I dated girls *and* continued to be attracted to other men—physically, emotionally, intellectually, spiritually, socially, and sexually. Like many other young men my age, I was totally confused about the impulses and desires within me.

And it did not necessarily help that I grew up in white, middle-class America in the 1960s, 70s, and 80s. My response to "gay culture" was a mix of curiosity and repulsion. Knowing I was gay since early adolescence, I was curious about what it would mean to live an "out" gay life. But I had no one to talk to about it—at church, at school, or at home. I was repulsed by the stereotypical gay role models, usually men who were, more or less, raging queens ... not that there is anything wrong with that.

As a family, we were faithful in attending a nearby Presbyterian church every Sunday, and I was faithful in going to the church's youth group, trying to find my niche among other young people. But the relational and dating models that were held up to us as "normal" were all heterosexual ones; being a "homosexual" was clearly a "sin," and something to be denied.

Later in life, amid the confusing, scrambled message of the Church (Catholic and Protestant alike) regarding what is written in Leviticus concerning ancient Jewish temple cultic practices that condemn "crimes against nature" (the cultic mandates in Leviticus also leave out people with disabilities, menstruating women, and so on), and whether or not the Apostle Paul was referring to pornographic pederasty in Romans, I was saved by the Psalms.[2] I have a small, beautifully and artistically designed card of the words of Psalm 139:

> O Lord, you have searched me and known me ... it was you who formed my inward parts; you knit me together in my mother's womb ... my frame was not hidden from you, when I was being made in secret, intricately woven in the depths of the earth. Your eyes behold my unformed substance. (1, 13–16a).

3

Whether homosexuality is caused by a genetic code, by embryonic hormonal switches, or by a deep, complex, mystical propensity that is more subtle than "nature versus nurture," all I know is, first, that I have always been attracted to other men, as have millions of others through time. Second, God made me who I am and knows me through and through. I can do nothing to escape the presence of God in Christ. For me, the words of the psalmist confirmed to me that I am who I am by God's design. End of argument. The only time I got in trouble was when I denied this truth and embraced a falsehood. When I lied, was deceitful, hidden, or obtuse, I always got in trouble with others and myself. The grace of God in Christ that truly liberated me was shockingly bright and glaring, breaking apart the fragile and brittle veneer of my otherwise "safe" closeted heterosexual, white, middle-class American existence. With grace, God dashed and smashed my American dream. I held in my hands the remnant, now ashes, of what was once my carefully constructed, fabricated life. I now live more authentically.

HIDE AND GO SEEK

When I was young, I thought I was a master of games such as hide-and-seek and capture the flag. As a closeted gay man, I found these skills quite handy. I continued dating women in college, even though there were one-night stands and frequent encounters in other places with other gay and supposedly "straight" men throughout high school, college, seminaries, and graduate schools. The idea of even dating another man in college was foreign to my cloistered, white bread, suburban world. The idea of going against the grain was not in the script. Adherence to the script, obeying the script, living the American dream, in which those who worked hard and followed the rules were well rewarded, was my mantra.

I understood marriage based on my own family of origin: it was a mom-and-dad operation, with dad as the breadwinner, and mom being the stay-at-home wife. My former wife came from the same mold; this is how we understood being a family. In fact, living together *before* marriage was a big enough obstacle that we did not even consider that arrangement a possibility for us. We were fated to live the life of "husband and wife," in which the wife took the name of her husband at a church wedding. Civil unions? Same-sex marriage? These concepts weren't even in our vocabulary.

COME OUT, COME OUT, WHEREVER YOU ARE!

My emergence out into the brilliantly diverse community of gays, lesbians, bisexuals, and transgendered people was slow, mesmerizing, chaotic, hurtful, and celebratory. The majority of the senior faculty members at Duke Divinity School were outwardly hostile to gay and lesbian civil unions or marriages and to the ordination of gays or lesbians in the United Methodist Church. In the greater university community, I discovered that many of the university's lesbian and gay associate and full professors who had tenure were exhausted from fighting so many battles on campus, in the community, and nationally. They offered a limited amount of helpful advice on how I should proceed in the largely homophobic culture of Duke Divinity School.

With the help of a great therapist, time, and an incredibly understanding now-former wife, she and I separated for a year (North Carolina law) and then were divorced some time later. Unfortunately, while we were in the middle of the separation process, I was publicly "outed" and blackballed by a senior theologian at the Duke Divinity School, which cast a shadow over my application for tenure. After ten years of teaching at Duke, copious publishing, and receiving awards and rave reviews from my students, I was denied tenure. Was it because I am a gay man and there has never been an openly gay or lesbian person who has been on the faculty of this more than seventy-five year-old seminary?[3] For legal reasons, I'll let the reader decide.

Today—now divorced, still a father of two, though no longer a teacher at Duke—I dedicate *this* book to all of the average, ordinary, run-of-the-mill, slightly dysfunctional, healthily weird families that more or less resemble something like the family in which I grew up, once married into, and am still part of.

JOURNEYING ON A SLIGHTLY DIFFERENT PATH AND A VERY DIFFERENT WORLD

Being a gay dad means that the once-standard script I followed for being a father in American society is no longer valuable to me … or valid. I have been living improvisationally since I was outed and have grown into my role of being a dad who is gay. Although my progress has been slow at times, I have come to understand that there are different shapes and kinds of families—all based on the mysterious presence of love and a level of commitment that provides a steadfastness that helps in challenging times and guides us in our family celebrations. LGBT families have all had to do some trailblazing, being pioneers of sorts, because while we as parents do what all parents must—provide structure; love, assume roles, functions, and responsibilities; and engage in healthy patterns of communication—some of the way we live is unique to our kind of family.

Here's one way of describing what it feels like to be a gay parent in a largely straight-parent world. When I visit parts of New Zealand and Australia, they seem remarkably similar to the U.S., including the homes, streets, streetlights, people, clothing, bushes, grass, sounds, and American fast food. However, there are small, slight differences that remind me I'm not at home anymore: everyone drives on the right side of the car while driving in the left lane; the fast-food places that I know in the States have slightly different names in these other countries; when people talk, I understand the words, but the accent sometimes trips me up and I find myself asking them to repeat themselves.

So it is with being a gay parent. I'm okay watching my son on the soccer field along with all the other parents and siblings—that is, until I notice that I am probably the lone gay man on the sidelines except for one married father who keeps looking at me with flirtatious eyes. I am okay dealing with the teachers in my son's middle school until one of the female teachers shows an interest in me, and my son asks, "She wanted to know if you are single and available. Do I tell her you're gay, because she hasn't a clue?"

These moments and others like them are why I have to write *this* book. It is about getting through those awkward social situations that gays and lesbians confront daily in an American society that provides us with few or no roadmaps. You may not see it in the census statistics, but in casual conversations among gay and lesbian acquaintances, I am pleasantly surprised to see how many gay dads and lesbian moms there are in the States as well as abroad, from Australia to Europe, Africa to Asia. More gays and lesbians who were hidden in marriages are slowly but surely leaving their heterosexual marriages and "coming out," though some choose to come out as gay or lesbian and remain living in heterosexual marriages. More gays and lesbians, bisexuals and transgendered people are choosing not to hide behind a heterosexual marriage and are uniting in either marriage (Massachusetts and abroad) or in civil union, choosing to adopt, welcome a foster child into their homes, or have children through in-vitro insemination. Still others choose to remain single and welcome children into their lives.

As for me and my family, like so many others before me, I was in a heterosexual marriage, during which I became the father of two amazing children—a daughter who is in college, and a son who is fully engaged in the act of being a teenager—and have been in a significant relationship with a handsome man for over a decade. I understand now that there are more ways of being a healthy "family" in this world than any one person could ever imagine. I also learned that truthfulness, love, respect, and communication matter in making any family healthy and healthier.

ABOUT THIS BOOK

This book is not like many other "self-help" or "how-to" books on families. Unlike those books, this book is written from the perspective of someone who is trying to clear a trail upon which only a few other authors have dared to trod. Try as hard as I might, it has been hard for me to find books that speak to or from the perspective of my kind of family, in either the public libraries, university libraries, or bookstores.

To find books on lesbian- and gay-headed households, I have had to go to the gay and lesbian, LGBT, or sexuality studies sections in libraries or bookstores, passing by the sections where all of the other family handbooks reside. But aren't we more like than unlike other families in American society?

- When I do find the books, they are usually one of three kinds: the first category are the psychological, relational, family theory-based books on gay- or lesbian-headed households, like *Gay Fathers* by Robert Barret and Bryan Robinson, which focuses on relational and psychological aspects, while D. Merilee Clunis and G. Dorsey Green did something similar in *The Lesbian Parenting Book.*[4]

- The second category of books is often authored by lesbian-headed households, addressing issues of the various methods of becoming pregnant and the early hassles of raising young infants; few get beyond the diaper-changing stage of toddler care. One reason for this is because many of the early "pioneers" were lesbian-headed households, who had the capacity to become pregnant biologically, versus gay men, who became fathers primarily through previous heterosexual relationships, foster parenting, or adoption.

- The third category highlights stories of gay or lesbian families, such as Noelle Howey and Ellen Samuels's story in *Out of the Ordinary; Lesbians Raising Sons* by Jess Wells; *Lesbian and Gay Families Speak Out* by Jane Levy Drucker; *Reinventing the Family* by Laura Benkov; Dan Savage's *The Kid*; *Love Makes a Family* by Gigi Kaeser and Peggy Gillespie; and B. D. Wong's *Following Foo*. These are wonderful vignettelike stories, but they fail to address some of the daily issues gay and lesbian heads of households face.

Interestingly enough, most of the books fail to address the uniqueness of family: what life is like *after* the child or children are in our homes, making us parents and changing the very contours of being a family. This book will talk about life in the daily visited arenas of activity of a middle-class family. It is written in the context in which the Christian faith matters and is central to our lives, as does going to soccer practice, being active in school events, talking to teachers about grades, getting children into college, going to movies and skating events with kids from other families, having sleepovers, going on field trips with children's classes ... and the list goes on. It is to and for similar families, and for those interested in my kind of family, that I write this book.

So, what are the problems that some people have with gay, lesbian, bisexual, or transgendered couples who are parents or guardians of children? After all, my family life isn't all *that* different from when I was married: I still drive the same car; have a job;

have health and retirement benefits; am in love with my children, even on the days when we all get on each other's nerves; have bills to pay, errands to run, and project deadlines. But, unlike that of my divorced friends (who seem to have no problem announcing to the world that they are divorced), being gay in a world of acquaintances, friends, associates, and people whose faces I know but cannot remember their names, my situation is strangely different, both in how I now approach the world and how I am known by others. I am more self-confident in some circles, but strangely uneasy in other places where I would have been more comfortable when I was married. Likewise, with my friends, some of them needed time to recalibrate our friendship and reacquaint themselves with who I really am. In other words, it was one thing to know me as a straight man who was a dad and a husband; it is something else to know me as a gay man who is a dad and a longtime partner.

Being known as a gay man who is a dad has brought unexpected challenges that I never faced as a seemingly straight man who is a dad. There are the usually one-dimensional stereotypes of gay men that I face daily; for example, being effeminate; knowing lots of Broadway tunes; being in love with the albums recorded by Babs and Bette; a "friend of Dorothy"; not into sports; great interior designer; good eye for color; loathing growing old; and a bit overly critical, snobby, or "bitchy." Meanwhile, my sisters who are lesbians are described as flannel-wearing, Home Depot-shopping (unlike gay men who go to Lowe's), butch-looking lesbians, and K. D. Lang, Ellen DeGeneres, Elton John, and T. R. Knight aficionados. While some of these stereotypes may be true, there are plenty of straight men and straight women who find themselves liking the very same things that gay men or lesbian women do. While these one-dimensional stereotypes can be funny, especially in comedy clubs or on Comedy Central, they can be difficult to deal with in real life.

There are some issues that confront gay dads and lesbian moms that no one could have prepared us for, and those are the things I want to address in *this* book. I have found that prejudice toward gays and lesbians may not be overt, but is often expressed as extremely subtle digs or comments that can be very damaging not only to the psyches or the souls of gay or lesbian parents, but to their loved ones as well. Beyond the one-dimensional stereotypes that many people think define being gay or lesbian in modern society—*and* define gay- or lesbian-headed house-holds—many people in this country have additional biases that affect the larger society as a whole. But to paraphrase the ACT UP activists and Larry Kramer in the 1960s and 1970s: We're here as gay and lesbian parents; we're definitely queer ... so get used to it, already.

SPEED BUMPS ON THE ROAD OF FAMILY LIFE

As there are weird and silly characterizations or stereotypes of gays and lesbians, bisexuals and transgendered people, some that now carry mythic weight, there are also misunderstandings in our society that shape the impression some people may have of those of us who are gay or lesbian and who are responsible for raising children and caring for one another. William Lederer and Don Jackson's book *The Mirages of Marriage* contains a list of "myths" that reflects most people's ideas about being married.[5] As I read the list in family therapy classes, I realized how many of the "myths" I had bought into and acted on in my life—only because that was the way I was raised. One of the myths was the false assumption that people marry because they love each other; another is that most married people love each other; yet another, that love is necessary for a satisfactory marriage. The list goes on and on, and is well worth reading and contemplating for all couples, both straight and gay.

While family therapists write and talk about the dynamics of the relationships themselves, gay and lesbian parents face additional issues—societal dynamics that continually shape and sometimes distort our relationships. Some in the gay and lesbian community also argue that certain dynamics of our relationships are unique to gay and lesbian relationships and may not be present in heterosexual relationships. This is a valid concern that I will try to address as well. But I find that mischaracterization of who we are and our relationship as a gay couple is a creeping problem in my relating to my partner and to my children, and this has to be dealt with in this book.

Like Lederer and Jackson, I am also talking about "myths" and "false assumptions" about relationships, but, in this case, of others' misguided perceptions about those who are gay, lesbian, bisexual, or transgendered parents.

The other important feature of the book is that it focuses on the central aspects of family life *after* a child or children are part of the family system. In other words, unlike many other books on gay and lesbians families, this one will not cover how one can become a parent, including in-vitro fertilization, adoption, surrogate mothers, open adoptions, foster placements, heterosexual relationships, and the other inventive ways that gays and lesbians now find themselves parents.

Following are some of the issues I will address.

COMING OUT TO OUR CHILDREN

In the U.S., families are expected to have a mom and a dad, or the "parent" may be a single parent, a foster parent, a guardian, or a member of the extended family. And the assumption is that most of the mom and dads, single parents, foster parents, guardians, and extended family members are well-adjusted heterosexuals.

But, in reality, amid single-parent families in which a man or a woman may be the parent, or in families with a grandparent, aunt, or uncle who is head of the household, having a mom and dad, together or alone, is not necessarily the norm. However, as a first step, gays and lesbians who head households need to be aware that our children, and many of the parents of our children's friends, will take some time getting comfortable in knowing us as parents, depending on the communities in which we live.

The next step may be telling our child or children that we are gay or lesbian. It is an odd and awkward "rite of passage" that no heterosexual can truly understand, as we live in a world that does not expect such a public "outing" of heterosexuals. This is an important early chapter in this book, because a successful family life depends on how we tell our children who we are.

WHAT TO CALL MOM OR DAD ... AND HIS OR HER PARTNER

Typically, even in this modern day and age, it is assumed that the mom in the family is the nurturer, while the dad is the bread-winner. Old stereotypes die hard, and these about mom and dad have long, deep roots.

Once we are out to our child or children as being a dad who is gay or a mom who is a lesbian, the next challenge before us is to explain that not all families have a mom and a dad. An intriguing issue many gay and lesbian parents have to struggle with is the naming of family members. There are children's books such as *Heather Has Two Mommies* to address the situation. Other families may have two dads, and other books—such as *One Dad, Two Dads, Brown Dad, Blue Dads; Daddy's Roommate;* and *Gloria Goes to Gay Pride*—reflect the struggle of naming ourselves in relationship with one another, since we do not fit the stereotype of the heterosexual American family.

COMMUNITIES OF FAITH

Households of faith, churches, have traditionally supported and provided communities for families. Throughout the years, families have provided the cornerstones of churches; they often include not only an immediate family with mom, dad, and children, but the extended family as well. So families have supported communities of faith, and communities of faith have supported families.

But communities of faith, sadly, do not support *all* kinds of families. Many gay- and lesbian-headed households have been excluded from families of faith for one primary reason: the presence of a gay or lesbian, bisexual or transgendered parent or child. Religious communities have a great impact upon our lives as gay and lesbian parents. Whether we are Christian, Jewish, or Muslim, we will choose to be part of communities who welcome our families, and try to be in dialogue with those who would rather we either conform or leave. We will have to try, one person at a time, to be in relationship with those who have never met a gay or lesbian person, and show them, through our love, that we are pretty "normal," whatever that means. I will address the various passages of Scripture that are used as excuses for prejudice. More importantly, I will address how we can help our children read those Scripture passages critically and respond to others in a constructive manner.

SCHOOLS: OUR COMMON GROUND

Schools play an important part in the life of our children because schools are the common ground upon which children from a variety of backgrounds interact and learn from one another. The original intent of public schooling at the turn of the last century was that the public schools would be the great equalizer, giving equal opportunity to *all* children, regardless of race, ethnicity, gender, economic class, and later, disability.

What many gay, lesbian, bisexual, and transgendered students have learned is that the public schools have not been a great equalizer for them in terms of being a safe place to get an education. Facing harassment—verbal, physical, intellectual, sexual, and emotional—from teachers, staff, and students alike, LGBT students have been courageous in trying to change an environment that can be toxic for some.

But many children with gay or lesbian parents find the same or similar scenarios being played out in the public schools. While some have positive experiences finding other children with gay or lesbian parents, others have mixed experiences in schools as they explain to their classmates who their parents are and tell them about the other adult figures their family's life.

RUNNING A HOUSEHOLD

Who does what, when, and how in a family is always up for discussion and rearrangement in any household. It is the parents' responsibility to teach the up-and-coming generation, through word and deed, how to be part of a family.

But what does one do when the rules of engagement for being a family aren't the same as the traditional heterosexual model? This chapter focuses on control issues that arise in a blended family. In many blended families, there is usually some tension in determining boundaries, drawing lines of authority, and deciding what responsibility a parent's partner has for the child or children. While the lines of authority may be the same as in heterosexual families, social biases also tend to shape these relationships, even within a household.

SAME-SEX UNIONS AND GAY MARRIAGES

Having married several heterosexual couples in my lifetime, I am well acquainted with the bonding words of intent, the vows, and the sharing of rings. After all, marriage is only supposed to be between a man and a woman. There is nothing that can change that, is there?

How do gay and lesbian parents celebrate marriages, same-sex unions, or covenant ceremonies, and anniversaries, in a world in which same-sex unions and marriages are still relatively new? Whose celebration is it—who is in inside this "circle of celebration"? How we celebrate our unions is a great opportunity for our children to understand the many ways of loving another.

HOLIDAYS

Holidays revolve around the nuclear and extended family. Think of it: Thanksgiving, family reunions, Christmas and Passover—extended family gathering. New Year's Eve? Easter? Memorial Day? Fourth of July? Labor Day? Family, family, family.

In a country that likes to shape secular holidays and religious holy days around the heterosexual nuclear or extended family, as with other celebrations in our lives, we find an opportunity to do something new and different as we negotiate with our children and other loved ones about the "meaning of the season" of holidays and religious celebrations.

FRIENDS ... AND THEIR PARENTS

One of my children wants to have a sleepover at my house. That's fine. I ask whichever child wants the sleepover to ask the other child's parents if we have permission for the child to sleep over. Usually the answer is "sure, that'll do!" Or, if the sleepover can't happen, it is usually because of a schedule conflict.

What do we do when the other parent's child says "no" because I am gay? An awkward aspect of being a child in a lesbian- or gay-headed household is with a child's friends and his or her parents. There are numerous times that a gay or lesbian parent has been the reason that a child's friends cannot come and spend the night, because the child's friend's parents refuse to allow him or her to spend the night in the same house with a gay or lesbian person.

LEGAL POTPOURRI

With marriage, a couple receives benefits just because they are being wed within a certain state in the United States. As a pastor for weddings, I may add the line, "By the laws of the State of (fill in the blank)," and the couple is married, but only after the marriage license (contract) is signed.

What do you do without laws that cover a gay or lesbian couple? This short section will focus on the issues we all need to address in gay- or lesbian-headed households in terms of legal protections and rights, including adoption, joint physical and legal custody of children with one's former spouse in case of a divorce, living wills for medical reasons, receiving a partner's benefits, powers of attorney, and real estate and property laws.

As I trundle down the pathway of life, sometimes talking with my partner and/or one of my children, smooth sailing for most of the way, something comes up and surprises me, slows me down, and causes me to think about how we, as gay dads and lesbian moms, and our families, are treated and related to in this world.

While I would like to discuss these situations from the point of everyone who is openly bisexual, transgendered, or questioning, I cannot do everything in this book, but hope that the reader can translate the book's insights into his or her own experience.

For readers who are from a "family of origin" or extended family members or those who are neither gay nor lesbian but know someone who is, thank you for reading thus far. Thankfully, with groups like PFLAG (Parents and Friends of Lesbians And Gays), we have opportunities to learn from each other.

GETTING REAL—OR BEING PUSHED INTO REALITY

So what happened to the *other* book, the one about the "normal American family"? It's a simple yet painful answer: real life interrupted. The book I began writing years ago can no longer be written by me. I am now living a family life vastly different from the book I had first proposed. The book that demanded to be written, this book, comes out of the life I am now living and the need for information that I have seen firsthand.

1

❧

COMING OUT

"I'M GAY!" "MOM, DAD ... I'M GAY!"

"HONEY, I'M GAY!"

"KIDS ... YOUR DAD IS GAY!"

Telling them was as hard in some ways as I had anticipated ... my eldest (though) said "Oh, mother, we've known for years."

—COLONEL MARGARETHE CAMMERMEYER, RET.[1]

A BIZARRE "UNOFFICIAL" OFFICIAL RITE OF PASSAGE

As a pastor, I have a deep respect for the power of rituals. Leading worship Sunday after Sunday, I have been moved by the power of rituals to shape the collective action of a group of people who come from all kinds of backgrounds and histories. Our personal stories are suddenly put on the "back burners" of life, and on the front burners, we focus upon the corporate, communal gestures of being the body of Christ in the flesh. When I celebrate the Eucharist, I am fully mindful and in awe that the words I am repeating are, literally and figuratively, as old as the Church. When I baptize infants during worship, I recognize that their parents and I are part of a great lineage of other disciples in the midst of a greater throng of people (saints here and above) who "baptize them in the name of the Father and of the Son and of the Holy Spirit" (Matt. 28:19).

In families large and small, as well as in corporate gatherings, clubs, support groups, and communities of faith, we understand that rituals have a way of shaping us as a group and as individuals as we have ways of shaping rituals in our communities of significance, like families and communities of faith.[2] For example, on the one hand, when we participate in the religious ritualistic practices of the Jewish or Christian faith, our identity as "Jew" or "Christian" is shaped and nurtured. In the Christian tradition, we know we are the body of Christ through the liturgical rituals of worship, including the praying of prayers, the recitation of Scripture, the communal confession of sins, and active participation in the sacraments of Eucharist and baptism. These rituals and their elements remind us of who we are—Christians—and whose we are: God's own people, and co-pilgrims with Christ.

On the other hand, the rituals that we practice are passed down, generation to generation, and change within generations and among cultures. They are, after all, mostly human inventions. In the Christian tradition, the Church took the Old Testament prophet John's ritual of baptism and, based on the baptism of Jesus, made it a Christian rite of passage into the greater life of the Church. Likewise, the eucharistic celebration mirrors elements of the Jewish Passover seder meal in which Jesus took the unleavened bread of Passover and a cup of wine and reconfigured and blessed their elements. The meal became a communal supper that continues to shape and nurture those who desire fellowship with one another in the spirit of Christ.

As Christian communities have rituals that are commonly referred to as "rites of passage" into a body of believers,[3] those of us who are gay, lesbian, bisexual, or transgendered also experience ritual. One of the first, strangest, almost bizarre, "unofficial" yet necessary rituals of growing up GLBT is what has commonly been referred to as "coming out" to one's family members, friends, associates, and even people we do not even know. For many, this is where the journey of being GLBT starts, with the day that one comes out to the world. Coming out is a rite of passage that is specific to gays and lesbians but not to heterosexuals. I have never heard my children tell me they are straight, but most people who are straight do not have to "come out" and tell his or her parents that he or she is not gay or lesbian. Such is the power of being in the majority versus those of us who are in the minority.

The reason for this coming-out ritual? Most census records and statistics[4] show that up to 98 percent of lesbian and gay people were raised in heterosexual/straight-headed families. With the rise of more gays and lesbians being in coupled, long-term relationships and having children (80 percent of gay and lesbian couples stay together for over a year[5]) and bearing children (either through adoption, medical intervention, former heterosexual relationships, or foster guardianship), there will be a slow decline in this overall number. Thus, the vast majority of LGBT people have gone through this "coming out" ritual or rite of passage.

What is it that we are "coming out" from? In the LGBT community, the common reference is to the "closet" in which we have hidden. Granted, there are the somewhat cynical jokes that we were in the closet because we loved the clothes, but in a very real sense, we were in the figurative (if not literal) closet in our households because we were hiding. We were hiding from ourselves, hiding from others, from God, and hiding from the world. We did not want to be found out, because we were either embarrassed or ashamed. The image of the closet is powerful, for in all variations of games of "hide-and-seek" played indoors, the closet is one of the best places to hide when you don't want to be found. Coming out is literally and figuratively not wanting to be in the proverbial "closet" anymore, breathing stale air, feeling uncomfortably stuffy because of all the clothes—and other souls—who are not able to figure out how to get out.

The courage to come out of the closet, to be found, to tell the world who we are, should not be belittled or rushed. While some people are, unfortunately, pushed out of the closet, many people come out of the gay closet when they feel or sense that it is the right time, among the right people, in the appropriate context.

Here is the literally "bizarre" part of the ritual of coming out: sooner or later, we who are LGBT "come out." Yet, unlike all the rituals and traditions of a church or synagogue, which are written in books with extensive commentaries on each and every nuance, there is no official manual or even a pamphlet. Even for family rituals, there are self-help books that provide such guidance. There is nothing in the LGBT section of bookstores or libraries that specifically tell us "How To Come Out to Family and Friends in Five Easy Lessons," with various options, tactics, and suggestions.[6] The places we learn about the process or rituals of coming out are through books, movies, DVDs, television miniseries, and, in a serendipitous way, from our friends or other LGBT people.

Is coming out and living honestly and openly necessary? Yes, for our own spiritual, mental, emotional, and physical health. Living truthful lives—like our straight friends and acquaintances do—reduces the kinds of stress that can impede good health. And while there are too many books to name that tell us that our mothers (but not fathers) always knew we were lesbian, gay, bisexual, or transgendered, from personal experience, I can say that many mothers, as well as fathers, may have had the intuitive sense that something was "different" about us, but many parents preferred to bury this information deep in their subconscious than deal with the reality that their child was not straight. Denial is common for LGBT people and for our family and friends.

In most families, there are at least three elements of the coming-out process: first, coming out to one's self; second, coming out to one's significant other (perhaps a spouse or parents); and third, coming out to the children. Even if a child is born within the context of having two moms or two dads, because the majority of the world is composed of people who are straight, children will, sooner or later, ask why their household is a little different from someone else's family at school, in church, or on the playground.

COMING OUT TO ONE'S SELF

The first person I had to come out to was myself. Coming out was a slow process, and being honest with myself only happened by being honest and open with others in my life. Being open or coming out of the closet to yourself is like looking in a mirror and saying "I'm queer,"[7] which is a good first step. But the real test is being out to someone else. In my case, I looked in the mirror once and said to the visage looking back at me, "You are gay; you are a faggot; you are a big ol' homo; you are a radical faerie; you are queer as they come; you make new marks on the Kinsey scale." But my coming out was validated and gained the weighty heft of truth and honesty when I came out to my partner Dean. Being fully open with him that I was gay was also the way that I was open with myself that I am gay ... call it double-involvement or double-revelation.

It is in relationships and fellowship with others who are gay that I also came to understand that God created me to be who I am: a son of God, loved by Christ, accompanied by the Spirit, who also happens to be gay. Coming out to Dean and to myself was also coming out to myself in God. Granted, I had prayed long and hard, asking God to take away this desire to be with other men, to make me straight and date women. This is what I had been taught in groups like Young Life and Inter-Varsity when they covered sections of high school and college life, respectively: to be a normal, God-loving and God-fearing Christian man was to be straight and date women, marry a woman, and have children with her. Their theological anthropology was the closet that I cowered in. In such Christian groups, I did not need anyone else to create a closet for me: I built my own closet and fortified it, thanks to the assistance of others in these groups. But it was also in these nondenominational evangelical groups that I met other closeted LGBT people, equally cowed into closets of their own making. Thus, it took a community of people to build a closet, and it took a community of people to deconstruct it.

One caveat: once I was out of the closet of homophobia (which is the timber of these closets), I have been surprised at how often the closet reconstructs itself, and I am again forced to come out, be open, admit with a right amount of pride (not the kind that is vice driven) that I am a son of God—and gay. It seems that for my lifetime I will be known as the gay pastor.

COMING OUT TO ONE'S SIGNIFICANT OTHER

This isn't always the case, but for some of us who have either been dating or were married to someone of the opposite sex and sexual orientation, this is a crucial next step in the concentric rings of "coming out": coming out to those close to us.

For me, seeing and being around more gay and lesbian couples, along with being in love with Dean, made me realize that something had to give and something had to change. My wife Pam was aware of my attraction to men and their attraction to me, but neither of us talked about it much through the years, except for certain times in which my relationships with specific men seemed to take my time, energy, and attention away from her. I was simply and matter-of-factly in love with most of these other married men, and they with me, but because we were both married and scared, I always returned home. To some, I used Pam as a "skirt to hide behind," which may be true. I have found that the courage to be open and honest is more rare and special than I thought, especially when I am around not only gay dads and lesbian moms who are out, but as I watch the awkward dance and games that hidden gays and lesbians still play.

COMING OUT TO ONE'S PARENTS

My mental image of someone coming out to his parents, gleaned from scores of films and books, usually involved sitting in a living room, dining room, or parlor (if European or English). The young man sits across from his mother and father, and says something monumentally simple, such as "Mom, Dad, I'm gay." Then either there is a burst of tears from the mother, who covers her face as the father runs away angrily, or both parents look down at the floor and quietly say, "We thought something was going on, but didn't know how to ask about it." But sooner or later, with or without the help of a therapist, the family comes together again and deals with "it," the "it" being the homosexual condition of the beloved son.

These scenarios seem, well, easy and systematic. I was forty years old when I finally came out to my former wife, my parents, and my children. It was my now-partner Dean who encouraged me to come out to my parents during a Christmas vacation. First, I came out to my mom in the car while driving to pick up one of my children from a play date. She reminded me how she almost had me see a therapist when I was in college. She demanded that I tell my father, too. Later, we were all sitting around the living room, drinking wine. With my former wife and my mom waiting, I remember digging my cracker into soft cheese and saying, "Dad, I need to tell you something important to me, and us: I'm gay."

No lightning bolt, though the room was silent. He asked my mom, "Did you know about this?" She answered that she did. His concerns included how we were doing, what would happen with the children, and, for my dad, the eternal concern: how would this revelation affect my retirement and health benefit package from Duke.

Then Dean and I took my parents out for coffee at a nearby health-food store for a cup of coffee and gave them permission to ask any question they had under the moon, stars, and sun about our relationship or about my being gay. This allowed us to share our thoughts and feelings openly and gave us permission to discuss our frustrations and sadness. Finally, we resolved some old hurts and wounds caused by my keeping the secret that I am gay.

And now I had to tell my children.

COMING OUT TO ONE'S CHILDREN

Unlike many gay and lesbian young people, as a father in his forties, my coming out was slightly different from that of a younger person. Getting through the first three tiers of coming out—self, spouse, and parents—was one thing. Telling my children that I would be moving out, that life would be a different because daddy is gay, was moving into uncharted waters. I did not have any stories, narratives, maps, checklists, or guideposts to figure out to handle the telling or to predict their reactions would be.

By the time we sat down with our children, I had moved out of the master bedroom that I shared with Pam and was now sleeping in the downstairs guest bedroom. The children knew that I had moved out of the bedroom I shared with their mom. Adrianne was seven years old, and Parker was four. I had heard from others and had read in several books that the earlier you tell children that a mom or dad is lesbian or gay, the easier it will be on them. As the rest of this book will show, this was not quite what happened.

Adrianne remembers that when I told them that I was going to be moving out and that I was gay, it was one of the few times in her memory that I had cried openly. Parker was too young to know what was happening and had adjusted to the daily and weekly routine of Mommy and Daddy living apart for most of his life. Pam and I stressed that we both loved them, even though we would not be living together. We have kept "on" this message through the years, letting the children ask me, my partner, or their mom any and all questions pertaining to our love and care for them.

At one time, my mom wanted me to stay in the marriage and not tell the children that I was gay until they both graduated from high school. The reason? To protect the children. But as I told her then, there would be times as they grew up through middle and high schools that I would ask them to be honest and forthright with me about what was going on in their lives. I could not imagine turning to them when they were graduating from high school and saying, "By the way, I have been living a lie for all these years. While I love your mom, I am gay."

CHILDREN OF GAY AND LESBIAN PARENTS COMING OUT

In recent years, many children of lesbian and gay parents have come out to the world. Some of them are calling themselves "queerspawn," telling the world around them that their parent or parents are gay or lesbian. I read somewhere that one child decided that, like his lesbian parents, he is going to change the world for gay and lesbian people "one homophobe at a time."

Our children also experience the emotional and spiritual weight of having to "come out" too, and this is not to be taken lightly. I have asked and will continue to ask my children if it is all right that I call them by their names in books and articles, or if they'd prefer pseudonyms; they emphatically say, "Of course we want you to use our real names!"

∾

As always, I am surprised at the resiliency of children and families. Even though honesty seems to be a rare quality these days, when people are taking the courageous step of "coming out," even when it may be painful for some to hear or grasp, the virtues of courage, self-control, and respect should be recognized in that process.

While there is not a one-size-fits-all strategy for coming out— or for any of the other issues or themes in this book—below are some pointers that may be helpful in the process of coming out.

STRATEGIES FOR COMING OUT

What works for this unscripted ritual of coming out in which LGBT people participate, voluntarily or involuntarily?[8] Consider the following strategies:

1. *Coming out to one's self and others takes enormous courage.* There is no doubt that coming out to anyone, especially to family members and close friends, is not easy, and only the individual who is gay or lesbian can do it. No one else can do it for us. Sometimes, if there is someone else who understands the background of the person who is coming out, the person who is coming out can ask for his or her company in the process, but it falls upon the individual to come out.

2. *Practice saying "I'm gay." "I'm a lesbian."* Some friends of mine have found that it actually helps to practice saying "I'm gay" or "I'm a lesbian" in front of a mirror. Practicing coming out in a quiet setting may not be a bad idea.

3. *Tell the children!* What I learned is that children are never too old or too young to learn that their parent(s) is gay, lesbian, bisexual, or transgendered. This doesn't mean that we have to tell them *everything* about our lives, but they should be helped to understand that God made each of us, and some of us God made to be straight and some God made to be gay or a lesbian. It is best not to wait for your child or children to initiate this discussion.

   If there is a spouse involved in the decision to tell the children, it is helpful if both are present during the discussion, showing a "common front," as it were, and letting the children know that both mom and dad want them to have this information.

4. *Share the story of your life.* What will be important to remember is that all we can do is share the story of our lives in a way that is real and sincere when we are ready to tell it. There should be no shame, guilt, or fear in telling the story, even though some people in our lives would like us to feel ashamed or guilty for being gay. The feeling of being afraid comes from our fear of how other people may react. We simply cannot control how other people will react to our honesty and openness. That is something the other person will have to confront.

5. *Help your loved ones discover that there are many ways to love.* In my coming out, my children, along with other members of my family, learned about a way of loving that they may not have known about or dealt with before. I also discovered that some of my friends and family members never knew that they felt bigotry toward gays and lesbians until I came out. What I tried to explain to all of them is that there are many ways to love other people. By "love," I mean the usual repertoire of Greek terms: *philia,* the love of friends; *agape,* the self-giving love of Jesus; *eros,* the romantic love found between two

people. Some people discover love in straight relationships, while others find love in gay relationships. Still others discover love in other forms of relationships, for example, fraternal love in the context of religious communities. My children now know about more kinds of love between women and men because of my coming out as a gay man.

6. *Be prepared to answer questions such as: If you're my dad, and you're gay, am I gay too?* This question has not come up with my children. Parker and Adrianne have informed me more than once, "Don't worry, I'm not gay," and I take their word for it. This is their "coming out" to me. But being out and gay, as would be true for lesbians, bisexuals, and transgendered people, is also an open invitation for further discussions, such as, "What makes a person gay or lesbian, bisexual or transgendered?" and "Who else can I talk to about this?"

7. *To be an "askable" parent, follow this checklist.* Authors D. Merilee Clunis and G. Dorsey Green suggest an easy checklist for gay and lesbian parents to use when telling and reaffirming with our children what it means to be children of a gay or lesbian couple:[9]

   □ Be knowledgeable: know beforehand some ready-made answers and responses to their questions;

   □ Be trustworthy: know that our children are relying on us not to be lying;

   □ Be brief: tell the children as much as they want to hear, not what we want them to know;

   □ Be clear: no big words allowed, or interesting academic discussions, or relying on case studies;

   □ Be respectful: children may not quite understand or agree with us: respect them;

   □ Be willing to revisit the topic, day or night.

The accompanying issue of coming out is, "Once I'm out, then what? How will it affect not only my life as a gay or lesbian person, but the life of my family? And what will happen to my friendships?"

The focus of the next chapter is on the immediate and extended family, and how being out and gay or lesbian may only be the latest evolutionary way of being a family in the long, confounding, weird story of "family" in the human race.

2

⌘

WHAT TO CALL "MOMS,"
"DADS," AND "PARTNERS"
... IT'S ALL IN THE FAMILY

I was adopted by a gay couple, and one of my fathers is Irish, and his grandmother's name was Hollahan, so rather than choose one of their last names, or give me both, they gave me an old family name of one of my dads, Hollahan, which is Irish, like my dad. But I'm not Irish.

—DAN SAVAGE[1]

AH, FATHERS' DAY!

In 1909, in the small city of Spokane, Washington, Sonora Smart Dodd was listening to a Mother's Day sermon. The sermon inspired her to have a special day dedicated to her father, William Jackson Smart, who had brought up her and her siblings single-handedly after their mother died. The idea soon caught on and, in 1924, President Calvin Coolidge supported the idea of a national Father's Day based on Dodd's petition. In 1926, a National Father's Day Committee was formed in New York City.

However, it was thirty years later that a joint resolution of Congress recognized Father's Day. Another sixteen years passed before President Richard Nixon established the third Sunday of every June as a permanent national observance of Father's Day in the honor of all good fathers that contribute as much to the family as a mother, in their own ways.[2]

When I was growing up and buying my father and grand-father "Father's Day" cards at Hallmark or other card shops, the cards usually had an image of a dad driving or washing a car, smoking a pipe, wearing a tie, hanging out with his pretty little wife, mowing the lawn, fishing, playing a sport, or performing other "manly" tasks, functions, and responsibilities. There were no images of a father playing with his children, ironing clothes, watching a Broadway musical, dancing, painting a child's portrait, cooking, cleaning, or indeed any words that would be appropriate or fitting for a gay dad.[3] As for looking for the right card that would fit my partner Dean, known affectionately to my children as either their gay nanny, Dad's partner, or their step-dad, after exhaustive searching, we have found no "right" card. The available commercial cards aren't appropriate either for a gay dad or for his partner. I can only assume that this is true for lesbian moms as well. In the end, we all resort to finding cards with interesting pictures that are blank inside or my children make their own cards and present them to us on Father's Day.[4]

WHAT DO WE CALL HIM?

The issue of finding a Fathers' Day card for a gay dad and his partner is preceded by the tension of figuring out what my parents and my kids would call Dean. Gays and lesbians in relationships struggle with nomenclature all the time. Are we living with a "partner"? It still seems funny to call each other that. "Lover" and "husband" seem appropriate at certain times, but partner fits most of the time. Some will ask me, "How's your husband?" and I still have to think about whom they are talking about. While the world of "husband and wife" is the context in which I grew up and I was publicly introduced as one-half of that couple at my wedding to my now former wife, there has been no public declaration of me and my partner as "husband and husband."

My partner, my significant other, goes by the name of Dean. A North Carolinian born and bred, he came into a relationship with children. While he had no interest in being a dad, he has welcomed my children into his life and loved them simply as Dean. Likewise, they have welcomed him into their lives, knowing and loving Dean for the good man that he is.

With Dean, we have gone through the struggle of "What shall we call Dean, Dad's partner or a step-dad?" They then turn around and with glee just call him "the gay nanny." Of course, this is complicated by what we call each other and, since marriage is not allowed among gays and lesbians in North Carolina, we do not call each other "husband" or "spouse," but "partner."[5]

My children regale their friends with what they did over a weekend, mentioning going to a movie or going out to dinner with Dean, or shopping for clothes with Dean, or being picked up by Dean to go to an appointment. With Dean, they can complain about their mother and father and know that he is one who will always listen to them.

My children have struggled with explaining Dean and their dad's relationship, not always sure what they can say or how to explain it. Consider the following discussions I have had with the children. Parker, my youngest child, is currently in middle school as I write this. He tells me that it is "kind of strange trying to tell your friends that you have a step-dad, but that your step-dad isn't your mom's husband. When they get that, they think, 'That's weird; that's gay, like that's a bad thing, when it really isn't.' The most recent occasion for calling Dean "step-dad" came during Parker's promotion from middle school to high school when Dean, without knowing it, was introduced by Parker to his friends as "Dean, who is my step-dad, and this is my mom, and this is my dad," without explaining who Dean was in relationship with. The common assumption—because of the politics and rituals of marriage—is that being someone's step-dad comes about because the mother remarried after a divorce, and the new man she married is thus the step-dad. This even caught Dean off guard at the time.

Welcome to the world of "create-a-family," in which all the old rituals and the way things worked in "traditional," nuclear families is changing. Everything is up for grabs for gay dads or lesbian moms. Beyond just creating our own Father's Day cards, we are constantly making things up as we go along, including the roles and functions of who does what and when in a family. From whom you wake up with in the morning, who cooks, who cleans, who tends to the yard, who is the "breadwinner," to who handles the checkbook, all the roles and functions of the family are being reconfigured. Our families no longer fit North American stereotypical norms. What this chapter and indeed book is dedicated to is reinventing and reimaging the family, beginning with names!

WITHOUT KNOWING IT, I'M PART OF THE GAYBY BOOM

When you are young and married in American society—heck, in most societies—there is the heightened expectation that bringing children into the world is part of the routine. Even though the Protestant and Catholic churches have denounced gay and lesbian unions and marriages on the biblically unfounded and biased claim that "it takes a mother and a father to raise a child," modern society in general seems to assume that *all* newlyweds will, sooner or later, bring children into the world.

While we had given ourselves plenty of time to have kids, wanting to finish most of our educational goals, my former wife and I have always rejoiced and celebrated the lives of our children, who have enriched us in innumerable ways. What I did not know when we were starting our family was that we would soon be part of a "boom" of younger lesbian and gay people with children. Often called the "gayby boom," the trend for lesbian and gay couples in the past decade or so has been to become full-time parents. Bearing children, of course, is nothing new. What is novel is that many gay and lesbian couples have become families and are letting the world know it.

Once a gay or lesbian person is "out" to him- or herself and to his or her family, what happens to the rest of the family? After all, as has already been mentioned, my being an openly gay man has not only had implications, and in some cases recriminations, that affect my life; my children, as well as my partner, former wife, parents, former in-laws, brother (and the list is exhaustive) are themselves marked by having a ex-husband/son/ex-son-in-law/ brother who is out, gay, and is not ashamed or unhappy with life.

WE'RE HERE: THE CURRENT STATE OF AFFAIRS FOR GAY- AND LESBIAN-HEADED HOUSEHOLDS

The pilgrimage of lesbian and gay couples and heads of households being out and visible has been an interesting journey. Against federal, state, and local politics, gay and lesbian couples have been creative and have made due with whatever strands of laws and statutes they can find, and have woven a fabric of legal protection for ourselves and for our children. For example, in 1996, the U.S. Senate and House passed and President Bill Clinton signed a federal law known as the Defense of Marriage Amendment (DOMA), which stated that marriage was between a woman and a man thus making any other union less than a marriage. Moreover, in the 2000, 2002, 2004, and 2006 election cycles, many states passed amendments to state constitutions stipulating that marriage was between one man and one woman, thus outlawing same-sex marriage.

However, in 2004, the Supreme Court of Massachusetts said that marriage may be between two men or women, which prompted other states to pass amendments against same-sex marriage. At the time of the publication of this book, the states of Connecticut, New Jersey, and New Hampshire have joined Vermont in passing laws allowing civil or same-sex unions. Meanwhile, in Canada, along with countries like England, the Netherlands, and Spain, gays and lesbians have permission to marry, and can be in same-sex relationships legally in other countries.

Between 1977 and 1983, 40 to 60 percent of gay men were in long-term relationships, while 75 percent of lesbian women were in long-term relationships; of these relationships, 80 percent had been a "couple" for over one year.[6] The national average length of a gay or lesbian relationship is six years, and the national average length of a heterosexual relationship is seven years.[7]

While it is often hard to get an accurate reading on how many families have gays and lesbians who are heads of households because many lesbians and gays often live in places where the neighborhood or city may be less than "friendly" once the gay or lesbian couple are out in the open, nonetheless, the older statistics show a solid minority of gay and lesbian families who are willing to be public about their family life. Also, although this is a hunch with no statistical verification, there may be a few more gay- and lesbian-headed households with children than currently portrayed either in these older statistics or in more recent U.S. Census Bureau findings. The reality is that gay and lesbian parents and our children are here, present in America's neighborhoods, cul-de-sacs, urban hotspots, and rural farmhouses. And our numbers are growing.

A SHORT HISTORY OF FAMILIES

At Duke Divinity School, when I taught a course on the changing nature of families in the church, we would begin by "passing, kicking, and huddling" over the phrase "family values," which was the "political football" in some of the most recent elections. The common assumption was that there was agreement about what is meant by "family," that the definition has remained fairly stable from the dawn of civilization (which civilization?), and that "family" usually means a married husband and wife with their children (although the number of children fluctuates), with animals and some kind of vehicle for transportation.

Then we started to take apart and examine the word "family" more carefully, comparing "home" versus "household," throwing in a debate on "values," and concluded that the entire presupposition—the normality of the nuclear family—is simply the most recent way that North Americans understand family, but it is not normative for the rest of the world.

The first place we turned to was the "master narrative" or script that we follow when we need the definitive explanation of what we are doing or studying: the dictionary. I remember reading in one of the physician-writer Ferrol Sams's novels that he turned to the dictionary for the normative definition of "family" and found that there were eleven different ways of writing about it. Taking his cue, I looked at my *Webster's Collegiate Dictionary*. The first definition mentions nothing about a "man and a woman" or "mother and father" as the head of a family with children. It simply says, "A group of individuals living under one roof and usually under one head."[8] This is followed by ten categories of definitions, with many more subsets under each category.

Suddenly, the students were open to the possibilities of many different definitions of "family" and realized that the idea of family is context-dependent, meaning that each definition of family changes depending on the context or group of people who are defining family.[9]

Not only is the definition of family context-dependent, but the definition or description of family has changed throughout time. For example, as I will show below, what was considered a "family" or a "household" in the Old and New Testaments is different than how we think of them in modern North American society. Furthermore, these definitions also change in light of the economic, ethnic, racial, and multicultural prism through which we look at families.

So can't a gay man or lesbian woman—or couples—be the heads of households? And do children have to be included for a family to exist? If one is willing to be guided by the Holy Scriptures as interpreted by the community of faith, and if the words of Scripture have a relevance to them in directing our lives in contemporary society, then consider the following changes in family—according to a biblical norm—that may change lives throughout time and in different contexts.

DEFINING THE BIBLICAL FAMILY

In her book *Jesus' Family Values*, New Testament scholar Deirdre Good reminds us that the word "family" is alien to both the Old and New Testaments.[10] Our very modern concept of the family would not only have been unfamiliar to the patriarchs and matriarchs whose lives are chronicled in the Old and New Testaments, but unknown. Think about the following description of what we would consider a "family" or, as our biblical kith and kin would understand, a "household." As Rodney Clapp wrote in *Families at the Crossroads*, there is something seemingly "unbiblical" about the real, live, biblical families as recorded in both the Old and New Testaments.[11] Consider the following history and habits of family households:

OLD TESTAMENT: Families in the Old Testament defy the circa 1950s standards of being a healthy, normal family.

- *Polygamy:* It is important to remember that Abram and Sarai did not start out with children, which was not honorable in that day and age. Instead, Abram was given permission by Sarai to "know" (in the biblical sense) Hagar, who brought forth a son, Ishmael. It was not until later in their life, when Sarah and Abraham were older and Sarah was considered barren, that she bore a son, Isaac. Nonetheless, polygamy was considered—and still is considered by modern Bedouins—a legitimate practice.

- *More than one family under the roof:* What we would think of today as a "family unit" would include not only the "nuclear family," which sometimes consisted of a husband and wife if not a husband and a few wives, but the in-laws as well. Many parts of the family lived together in the nomadic world of biblical times. For example, Jacob's family and his sons all lived together on the same patch of earth, numbering up to the hundreds, as did Gideon's.

- *Children as small adults, bred for labor:* While we are currently under the spell of nineteenth-century German and English romantic vision of children as delightful humans who actually have a period of life called "childhood," the children in the Old Testament were seen as objects to be traded or swapped for labor purposes, reared and bred to take over the household's trade.

- *Tribe is thicker than water or loving feelings:* In the story of Ruth, there is a sense of surprise when we realize that Naomi, with the death of her sons, is all alone in the world. It is the magnanimous gesture of Ruth, the non-Israelite outsider, who saves Naomi from being completely alone as a widow, which was unheard of in that day and age, regardless of the feelings that people had for each other.

Of course, Mary and Joseph, the parents of Jesus, were bound by the traditions and customs of the Older Testament.

NEW TESTAMENT: Deirdre Good makes an important differentiation between *oikos*, which in Koine or early Greek meant "house" or "household," versus our understanding of family, and *oikia*, which refers primarily to the very architecture of a house or apartment, which sometimes slips into usage in describing the more sociological *oikos* understanding of household.[12]

Good's and Clapp's descriptions of the household help clarify the following:

- *Jesus challenges the nuclear family unit:* Rodney Clapp shows us that the family unit, as Jesus understood it, no longer simply included mom, dad, sis, and bro (and the house, car, and sundry pets), but *everyone* and *anyone* who is part of the realm of God's love. That means that our familial relationships in American and any society may be reconfigured in a myriad of ways because of the emergence of a new way of living in covenantal relationship with God. In Mark 3:31–35, Jesus is asked who are his mother and his brothers and, instead of pointing out Mary and James, who were in the crowd of listeners, Jesus instead turns the applecart of family systems upside down by saying, "Here are my mother and my brothers! Whoever does the will of God is my brother and sister and mother." This is the crucial determining variable for kith and kinship: "whoever does the will of God," even today, become our brothers and sisters *in the faith*. What Jesus is doing is making the biological relatedness of the Old Testament schematic secondary to the primary importance of doing and being about the will of God. And Jesus does this in the very company of his blood kith and kin!

- *Jesus condones violence, taking a sword against the American family:* In Matthew 10:34–38, Jesus speaks against idolatry or worship of the family unit: "Do not think that I have come to bring peace to the earth; I have not come to bring peace, but a sword ... whoever loves father or mother more than me is not worthy of me; and whoever loves son or daughter more than me is not worthy of me; and whoever does not take up the cross and follow me is not worthy of me." In this passage, Jesus states something that is quite painful for those of us caught in the American dreamscape to hear: Jesus, God in Christ, is more important than family ties. That is especially hard for many to hear in a Southern context, in which family roots matter so much. But in this passage, Jesus tells us whom we should worship, and it is not the family system we've grown up with.

- *Overthrowing child labor, Jesus blesses the little children:* As stated earlier, children were considered part of the economy, part of the labor force, as little adults in biblical days. In Mark 10:13–16, Jesus speaks of the little children, who were being shunted aside by the disciples, who thought of them as lowly as servants and slaves, and makes them key agents of change. "Let the little children come to me; do not stop them; for it is to such as these that the kingdom of God belongs" (Mark 10:14). Right up there with the peacemakers (Matt. 5), Jesus raises the status of children with this simple gesture of taking them up in his arms, blessing them, and enjoying them.

- *Paul's household of faith:* In Paul's letter to the church in Rome, Paul, echoing Jesus' new description of the family unit, writes that the Spirit of God has reconfigured our relationship with one another and with Christ through adoption! We are all adopted heirs of God, for by the Holy Spirit we have all become children of God: "You have received a spirit of adoption. When we cry 'Abba! Father!' it is that very Spirit bearing witness with our spirit that we are children of God, and if children, then heirs, heirs of God and joint heirs with

Christ—if, in fact we suffer with him so that we may also be glorified with him" (Rom. 8:15–17). Our primary household is no longer bound by our human born kith and kin, in which it is most often by blood that we are kith and kin. Instead, it is by the "blood of the Lamb of God," by Jesus Christ, that we are united and made part of the household of God.[13] This is why Paul can write to "us" consistently as "brothers and sisters," since in the Spirit of God, which is our primary bond, it is the way we can address one another. Such is the beauty and mystery of the *oikos,* the household of God.

- *The equality of ministry, women and men together:* In this household of God's own making and design, there is an equality among the sisters and brothers that was not shared among our Jewish forbearers. In Galatians 3:28–29, Paul writes that since we are now clothed with Christ, "there is no longer Jew or Greek, there is no longer slave or free, there is no longer male and female; for all of you are one in Christ Jesus. And if you belong to Christ then you are Abraham's (and Sarah's) offspring, heirs according to the promise." As we know, in the early Church, women and men shared in ministry, being elders and leaders even in their households.

While the Old and New Testaments have often been used as medieval cudgels to put us—gays and lesbians—in our second- or third-class space, when we look at the households described in the Scriptures, the 1950s model of the American family cannot be found. This comes as a great relief to me as a gay head of household, knowing that the biblical way of being a household has more to do with God in Christ than with modern American politicians and their "family values" football.

STRATEGIES FOR BEING A FAMILY

Some of the newfound freedom in reconfiguring and being family that this chapter may give us as gay- and lesbian-headed households are as follows:

- Being a family of "one man and one woman" is just one of many varieties of choosing and being a family in this world. We have the freedom and guidelines to reinvent and to be creative in deciding what kind of family we desire to be part of. And the beauty is that this is not only our choice, but a choice that can be argued as having biblical truth behind it.

- We still need some guidelines, models, master scripts, or narratives to show us ways to be family. No current television shows or movies show us the way. Some novels and self-help counseling books provide some pointers. For example, while many of us will come from families where moms and dads did certain jobs in the family, we will have to be creative in deciding what household chores we may choose to do that aren't prescribed by our gender or sex. We can be creative in the names we choose in our families. For examples, two moms can differentiate between the two of them by one being called "mom" and the other one "momma." Another gay couple chose not to go with "dad" or "father," but have the children call them by their first names.

- Because of the lack of information to guide us, it is important that we share our stories with one another, including both the high points and deep dark valleys of being part of gay- and lesbian-headed households.

- One issue at hand that has arisen in more than one family is that of a single gay or lesbian parent. If the single parent invites someone to sleep over in the family home, what should he or she call the date? Like any other single straight person who does the same thing, you'll have to figure this one out on your own.

- There is a misunderstanding that gay or lesbian parents may not be attractive to potential dates because we have children, otherwise known as "baggage." What I have come to understand is that *everyone* has some "baggage," though they may not say they do right off when first dating. I have met some wonderful gay men and lesbian women who would be interested in being part of an already-made family and who enjoy being part of a healthy-if-not-slightly-neurotic family.

- Lastly, we will need to be strong and courageous in trying new roles and functions in being family that may not be reflected in other family systems around us. We should come up with rituals that celebrate and honor the relationships we have in our family's life and celebrate often!

In being part of a lesbian- or gay-headed household, we will need to turn to some places of support for being a family from time to time. One of the more "natural" support communities is the Church. In the next chapter, the challenge is that of faith.

3

FAITH

Now faith is the assurance of things hoped for, the conviction of things not seen.

—HEB. 11:1

Don't tell me you're another one of those gay guys who've had sex with youth directors at their churches ... youth directors are the choreographers of Mississippi.

—KEVIN SESSUMS[1]

A PHONE CALL

Being a Christian by an act of God's grace, reminded by the Spirit regularly about this gift, being called by God in Christ to be an ordained clergyperson in a mainstream Protestant denominational church, and being a dad who is gay, I cannot express in words the hurt and bitterness welling inside me when I am almost daily assaulted with the swordlike words, comments, opinions, and assaults that day by day attack my very being from people who put "fish" stickers on their cars, trucks, and minivans and claim to be "God-loving and God-fearing" people. I shake my head in dismay regularly, wondering if we're reading the same Scriptures or worshiping the same God.

Consider "a day in the life of" account of what I can read or hear in just one day. As I was working on this chapter, a friend—another gay dad—called me at home to talk about something "awkward, but nothing serious" (his words). After a few brief seconds of playing catch-up with one another's lives and the lives of our respective children and partners, the something "awkward" was broached: what does one do with a cousin in his family who is a "conservative evangelical" who does not necessarily understand the "lifestyle," a.k.a., his being gay. My friend's cousin has been going around telling various family members about the "sin" of my friend's living in relationship with another man. My friend called me to ask, "What do I do in this situation? What verses can you steer me to in the Bible to make him think? What's my best recourse without hurting his feelings, but letting my cousin know that I have feelings, too?"

I opened up the newspaper in my hometown of Chapel Hill, North Carolina, *The Chapel Hill Herald.* The above-the-fold essay on the front page was about the major television networks not running an advertisement produced by the United Church of Christ that is pro gay and lesbian.

Elsewhere in the news, there is the story of the "former Rev." Elizabeth Stroud, who was convicted by an ecclesial judicial court of the United Methodist Church for being openly lesbian and living in a long-term relationship with her partner. Elizabeth was not only found guilty for being a practicing lesbian, but was subsequently defrocked. Many closet lesbian and gay ministers, priests, rabbis, and other religious leaders fear being outed in a religious community and institution that is hostile toward lesbians and gays, bisexuals and transgendered people.

Finally, on CNN this morning, June 27, 2007, there was a special on runaway, homeless gays and lesbians in New York City. The National Gay Lesbian Task Force estimates that 40 percent of the homeless teenagers on the streets in cities, towns, suburbs, and rural outposts are gay or lesbian youth. Why? Because many of them are told by their families to leave after they come out and tell their respective parents they are gay or lesbian. And many of these families are good Catholic and good Protestant families.[2]

BEING THE ROUND PEG AMONG THE SQUARE OPENINGS IN CHRISTIAN AMERICA

Simply being gay or lesbian is one of the most divisive issues in many religious or faith communities, be it Muslim, Jewish, or Christian. Some in this country say that the "gay and lesbian" issue has surpassed the "abortion" issue as the political football in this country's religious communities, but it still fits under the category of "family values" football. Granted, in each community, representative of each tradition, a person will meet those who are open and affirming of gay or lesbian people. There are lesbians, gays, bisexuals, and their straight allies who are trying to work within various religious communities to make them more open to and inclusive of lesbians and gays ... not only by welcoming gays and lesbians, but also by welcoming their families. Others are working towards the open ordination of lesbians and gays as ministers or rabbis or other leaders in religious life, while still others are fighting for lesbians and gays to be able to celebrate same-sex unions or marriages in their respective faith communities.

Likewise, in each faith community there are people who are either covertly or overtly against gays and lesbians. They are not only loud; they also seem to be media savvy and financially well off. And sometimes the group with the most money wins, as is true in many body-politic situations. Often, these people say something theologically cute and seemingly innocuous, such as "Love the sinner, hate the sin." On the surface, this seemingly shows that those saying it actually love all people, including unrepentant sinners: homosexuals, in this case.

What they actually mean, theologically and psychologically, is something that could be called "theological jujitsu." After all, we are all sinners in need of grace, seven days a week. What the comment means is that they will love or accept the person who is gay or lesbian as long as the lesbian or gay person is not sexually active; in other words, *not* in a fulfilling, loving, emotionally charged, intellectually stimulating, spiritually gratifying, and sexually active and meaningful relationship. The gay or lesbian person must be celibate or practice abstinence. Of course, asking someone to deny an important aspect of one's life—the physical, sensual, sexual self—is impossible. It is impossible to deny something that is so intrinsic to who we are: our bodies. It also fails to appreciate that "celibacy," as it is understood in the Roman Catholic tradition, is itself a calling or vocation, given by God to a few but not to all people.

To turn this logic around, how would a person who is straight and married or in a long-term common-law marriage like to be told that he or she is loved as a sinner, but "we just don't like the sin"—the sin being the heterosexual relationship, how the couple has sex. And imagine telling a straight couple that they cannot have sex.

Finally, imagine a world in which sex just doesn't occur. The argument gets downright silly.[3]

Some who are straight and openly against the ordination, let alone the marriage of gays and lesbians, claim that people who are gay or lesbian have an affectional disorder, a biological affliction, or are dealing with lingering insecurities from when we were children. In other words, gays and lesbians are simply replacing an emotionally missing same-sex parent with a contemporary of the same gender. So our affection for a person of the same sex is somehow an emotional disorder, an aberration caused by poor nurturing or social conditioning, something to be cured.

To deal with this "problem," gay and lesbian Christians of all stripes, including Mormons, subject themselves (or are coerced by loving families) to reparative therapy. This intense psychological experience tries to re-cast or resurrect the straight person who is hidden in the gay or lesbian person's body, psyche, heart, and soul. Much of the counseling, based on behavioral therapy, assumes that being gay or lesbian is not "natural" but is a psychologically aberrant behavior, and thus a choice that gay or lesbian people are consciously or unconsciously forced to make because of problems in their upbringing. The most visible person who went through this round of therapy was Ted Haggard.[4] Groups like James Dobson's Focus on the Family advocate reparative therapy in national conferences called "Love Won Out," in which there are speakers, musicians, and performers who gather together to convert those who are following the "homosexual lifestyle" or "sexual preference" into functioning straight people.

While there are many of the same issues confronting people in Judaism as well as among those of the Muslim tradition, I can only speak from what I know best and am part of, but I look forward to the dialogue that this book will hopefully generate. Furthermore, I come from the Presbyterian tradition, and this chapter will reflect that background as well—my apologies to those who are not of the Protestant tradition. Finally, for better or for worse, for "richer or poorer," the country where I write this book is one in which many people are quiet and submissive, afraid to put forth an opinion on gay and lesbian issues, while others are loud and vocal in their opposition.

While we are still striving to help people understand that we, just like "straight" people, were created in the image of God, it is important to remember that our children may suffer the worst from our living openly and honestly. They often are the recipients of the derision, bias, and discriminatory statements that we parents might not hear or receive. This is because "we adults" tend to forget the age-old axiom that our own mothers taught us, that "little pitchers have big ears." My children have heard many ugly things about gays and lesbians in general and about their own father in particular, from adults in our families. Unfortunately, such family members forget that children hear what they say and often repeat it to the gay or lesbian parent, out of fear for the life of the parent. Such words of bias do nothing but create havoc in the life of a family—unless we stick to the words "your problem is not my crisis."

THE BEACH HOUSE

To consider how blurred the lines can be between faith, religion, and politics, consider this story, from a friend whose daughter Brittney was the recipient of a grandfather's hatred toward gays in general and toward her father Bart in particular. Sixteen-year-old Brittney, a junior in high school, had gone with her mother and her mother's family to a beach house in California to beat the summer heat in the Stockton area of the state. Brittney looked forward to the cool ocean breeze coming onto the shore as she sat on the deck of the beach house, listening to her own music in her personal CD player.

On the first morning of the weeklong stay at the beach, the family gathered together for breakfast, one by one straggling into dining area, grabbing a bowl for cereal or popping bread into the toaster for toast. Coffee had finished brewing, and hot chocolate, milk, and orange juice were on the counter, with plenty of cups for the family members. As they all sat down at the table, the Pop-Pop of the family (meaning "grandfather" with a South Carolina accent) opened up the Bible (New International Version) for the morning's Scripture reading. Looking at the list of readings for the day from a Pentecostal Church list of daily prayers, Pop-Pop asked everyone to pray "Dear Father God," and then began reading the Scripture for that day.

Brittney dutifully listened to the Scriptures being read by her grandfather. She loved hearing his voice, knowing that resonant baritone belonged to someone who loved her. The prayer that followed the Scripture reading disturbed her: "Please be with the U.S. Senate as they debate passing a bill that would amend the Constitution, prohibiting gays and lesbians from ever being married ..." Brittney couldn't quite believe it. Brittney's father, Pop-Pop's former son-in-law, divorced Brittney's mother because he is gay and had decided that he could no longer live in a marriage and family that asked him to lie about who he is. Brittney took Pop-Pop's prayer to amend the Constitution as an attack on her father!

After the grand and final "Amen," again intoned by her grandfather, Brittney asked Pop-Pop for clarification about what he had prayed for. Pop-Pop told her that the U. S. Senate was going to vote on a bill to amend the Constitution, making it impossible for all lesbians and gays, like Brittney's father, from ever being married. Brittney saw it as nothing more and nothing less than an attack on her father. She was irate and saddened, and did not know what to say or where to turn. She hesitantly asked Pop-Pop why it was wrong for gays or lesbians to be married, and Pop-Pop told Brittney that it was simply impossible because God did not will that "Adam marry Steve, but be wedded to Eve. If God wanted Adam and Steve, He would have created Adam and Steve. But instead, he created Adam and Eve."

Mustering all of her courage, Brittney confronted her Pop-Pop carefully but persuasively, trying to get him to consider whom he was talking about: her father. Though it was a rather cold and malicious thing for Pop-Pop to do—to attack the father of his granddaughter—Brittney had the inner strength to confront such an authoritarian presence in her life and not back down.

Her grandfather tried to explain himself, but she kept at it, demanding answers but getting none that made sense. Pop-Pop understood, finally, what was going on: his granddaughter was not afraid to confront an older, supposedly wiser, man.

With a few tears in her eyes, Brittney and her mother spent some time later that day reading the Scriptures that have become central to the debate swirling around and among gays and lesbians in households: Leviticus 18:22: "You shall not lie with a male as with a woman; it is an abomination"; and Romans 1:26–27: "For this reason God gave them up to degrading passions. Their women exchanged natural intercourse for unnatural, and in the same way also the men, giving up natural intercourse with women, were consumed with passion for one another. Men committed shameless acts with men and received in their own persons the due penalty for their error." Brittney's mother wanted her to know the biblical basis for Pop-Pop's anger at Brittney's father. Sadly, Brittney's mother—who still harbors hurt and resentment from her divorce from her former husband—did not explain to Brittney how these passages could and should be read. Brittney was left clueless about how to read the Scriptures and frustrated with her Pop-Pop, who was angry at Brittney's dad because he had divorced Brittney's mother.

THE PROBLEM AND HOPEFULNESS OF SCRIPTURE

The Gordian knot that has been created out of the strands of religion and gays and lesbians is as thick and complex as it seems. There is no denying that the proverbial lines in the shifting sand have been drawn in churches—as well as presumably in the synagogues, mosques, and temples of this world—regarding what is considered within the bounds of proper living—in other words, discipleship in the Christian sense of the word.

Briefly, here are the strands of the knotty arguments that are made about gays and lesbians in the Church that stand in the way of our full and complete membership in a church. They also influence opinion and thus church law regarding ordination of open, "practicing" gays and lesbians as well as church marriages or same-sex blessings, and thus affect our families in the life of a congregation or parish.

- There is an ongoing debate regarding a series of Scripture passages from the Old and New Testaments that focus on the behavior or action of people in a day and age that is not our own. In his book *Jesus, the Bible, and Homosexuality*, theologian Jack Rogers names these eight verses:[5]

  1. Genesis 19:1–29, which is the story of Sodom and Gomorrah, and thus more about the issue of hospitality not being offered than anything else;

  2. Judges 19:1–30, rape of the Levite's concubine;

  3. Leviticus 18, which has to do with Jewish cultic law and the Temple;

  4. Leviticus 20, which also has to do with Jewish cultic law and the Temple;

  5. 1 Corinthians 6:9, which is a condemnation of vices generally;

  6. 1 Timothy 1:10, which is a condemnation of vices generally;

  7. Jude 1:5, 7, which is a condemnation of vices generally;

  8. Romans 1:26–27, which is about idolatry and no modern practice of homosexuality per se, based upon the cultural, normative practices of that day and age in the Roman Empire in the Greco-Roman culture.[6]

In all of these passages, they must first be understood in the historical, cultural context in which they were written, which would be either ancient Jewish, Middle East generally, or Roman contexts and people. For example, the

Romans passage is about Roman soldiers engaging in young male prostitution.[7]

Second, none of these Scripture readings is about the current practices of those of us who call ourselves gay and lesbian today and are living in long-term, significant relationships with people of the same sex. While these biblical verses all point to behaviors and human actions, the emergence of the "modern homosexual," involving one's mind, body, and psyche as way of being in this world, was legitimized in nineteenth-century Europe. Writers like Heinrich Hosessli, Karl Heinrich Ulrichs, and John Addington Symonds wrote essays and books discrediting their respective societies' condemnation of homoeroticism by arguing that it was accepted and encouraged in many of the advanced cultures like ancient Greece. By the end of the nineteenth century, even medical researchers were starting to see that being gay or lesbian is an age-old phenomenon that occurred more or less frequently in all civilizations.[8]

- One of my former colleagues at Duke University, Dr. Mickey Efird, always taught his classes in Old and New Testament studies that if "you read the Bible one way, then you've got to read the entire Bible that way." Ergo, if you read the Bible as a literalist, meaning that you read it with the eyes or goggles of inerrancy, that Scripture is infallible, then you must read the entire Scripture that way. If you read Scripture with an eye or practice of seeing the cultural, historical context in which it was written and read it with the eyes of faith, being capable of understanding how God could be making the Word alive today, then you must read it thoroughly in this fashion.

    If we read Scripture as Dr. Efird proposes, there is no chance of cherry-picking the Scripture verses that fit an argument that we want to make while ignoring the rest. Or of not living up to the expectations of the other parts of Scripture. For example, progressive magazine editor and social movement *Sojourner's* founder Jim Wallis often says that eight Scripture passages deal with something akin to gay or lesbian relationships, but many more verses deal with poverty and economics—but we ignore them. Or that Jesus made divorce ignoble, but that does not stop a lot of ministers or Christians from divorcing.

• Just as "It takes a village to raise a child," it takes a faith community to enable us or teach us to read the Scriptures. While there are debates among Christian denominations with different theological convictions about the interpretation of Scripture, what is evident is that just as we learn to read, write, do math, and think through teacher-student relationships, we are dependent on community in our reading and under-standing of Scripture.

What I have found is that often people read Scripture or hear about the above eight verses without ever talking to some-one about what they meant and could mean in this day and age. It is important to read and discuss such controversial Scripture in the community of faith, because it is foundational to much of what we understand as Christians in today's world.

• Jack Rogers points out that at times communities of faith have misused the Bible to justify being oppressive toward a group of people. In other words, the oppression that many of us who are LGBT are experiencing is nothing new, but is as old as the Bible itself. For example, biblical passages were used to justify slavery in the States during the Civil War as well as to justify abolition of slavery. And biblical passages were used—and continue to be used—to oppress women in the Church, denying women a place of leadership, whether as deacons or priests in the Catholic Church, or as ministers in some Protestant denomi-nations, for example, some Southern Baptist churches.[9]

What changes our biblical interpretation? Oftentimes changes in the mores or whims of the larger society cause reinterpretation. For example, with women making more strides in the workplace from the 1950s to 1960s, it seemed wrong and oppressive for women not to be ordained in most Protestant churches. That is why wider societal welcoming of gays and lesbians may finally push open the doors of many denominations and churches. As the polling shows, from Gallup to Pew, a growing majority of people in the United States not only accept gays and lesbians, but also same-sex marriages and civil unions.

- Faith, hope, and love abide (1 Cor. 13:13): It is imperative that we Christians who are gay and lesbian realize, especially when some throw Scripture at us as if it were a wrongfully used dagger (and I'm a pacifist) to hurt us or scare us into being "straight," that we do not worship the Bible per se, but Jesus Christ, the Son of the living God. While others treat Scripture as if the texts are sacred unto themselves, we need to remember that the words found in between the covers are important, but they are not God. God is God, and God is doing a new thing in which the Spirit keeps revealing glimpses of justice and love, which are keystones of the realm, the kingdom of heaven.

    At times, we all need to remember that the greatest command is this: "You shall love the Lord your God with all our heart, and with all your soul, and with all your mind. This is the greatest and first commandment. And a second is like it: You shall love your neighbor as yourself" (Matt. 22:37–39).

SUGGESTIONS

What are some things we need to consider or ask for as a gay or lesbian couple with children?

- *Baptism of our children:* This could be awkward for some churches and their respective pastors, priests, and ruling bodies, because if our unions are neither marriage or some other kind of union and we have children as "fruits" of our relationship, how can congregations bless the very children who are in a relationship that many see as, well, evil, sinful, or wrong? I have heard of some churches where the children were not allowed to be baptized because the parents were in a gay or lesbian relationship. All families left these respective churches.

  It is uncommon for churches to turn away children, let alone adults, from baptism. However, a church's ruling board and priest or pastor have a challenge on their hands. If our relationships are considered either sinful or wrong, how then can they bless and baptize the offspring or the adult? This may lead to an opening for further discussions.

- *Participating in the Eucharist:* Likewise, there are some churches who have turned away gays and lesbians simply because they are gay or lesbian. And gay and lesbian couples have been turned away from congregations simply because of their relationship and have never gotten to the point of receiving the elements.

  If this is ever an issue, it is important to stress that the Eucharist is meant not merely for saints of the church, but for all of us who remain quite sure that we are sinners. Our being cleansed, justified, and sanctified is not through our actions, but by the actions of grace fully unleashed upon the lives of Christians everywhere.

- *Marriage for all:* While this topic is covered in chapter seven, I need to take this opportunity, amid discussions of baptism and Eucharist, to stress that real marriage is for real people. It should be entered into with eyes wide open and with a readiness to grow in unexpected ways. Discussions of marriage for gays and lesbians are opportunities to engage the wider church in a discussion of marriage for all, gay and straight couples alike. After all, we live in an age of marriages performed in the name of God in Las Vegas that last merely a day, yet the couples receive all the rights and privileges not only of the state, but of the Church. And the quickie divorces do not seem to offend pastors or clerks in offices that hand out wedding licenses when they tally up the number of marriages. There is no limit in any state of the union for how many marriages one can have; one must simply be married to one person at a time.

- *Be active and be present in your local church:* It is important to "find a niche" in the local body of Christ, a church. For one's spiritual, emotional, intellectual, and overall health, it is important to find a place and people who not only welcome us and our families, but who are open to our participation in a church's life.

  When working with people with disabilities and churches who have or have not been welcoming, I have stressed the importance of finding a place that can either grow into our being present with the congregation or are already at a place and time in their history that *all* may worship, serve, laugh, cry, learn, teach, and be in fellowship with one another. But it will take an investment of our time, energy, and talents to hold the door open for others as well. It is, after all, a dance between our families and congregations, as it is for all families and congregations. In other words, as a pastor, I would give this advice to all families, gay and straight alike.

CHARGE AND BLESSING

At the end of worship, it is appropriate for the minister or pastor to send the congregation of pilgrims out with a cautionary word or charge to remember. Here is my charge to my readers. First, while lesbian and gay children learn the rites of deceit, impersonation, and appearance to hide who they really are because of shame and guilt, the church should be a place in which we do not have to practice these activities, for we serve a God who knows us and still loves us.[10] Being part of the body of Christ means that we strive for transparency and authenticity, not lies and secrets.

Second, I close with the vision of Deirdre Good, a lesbian in a same-sex, long-term relationship: "When I kneel side by side with someone whose construction of family looks radically different from mine, I witness to a God whose ways are not our ways, whose judgments cannot be limited by our finite understanding, whose generosity and creativity must not be circumscribed by our tiny hearts and minds."[11]

But God's imagination is not quarantined to the Church per se, but is all over the world ... including in schools. Let us now consider what is going on in our schools as we learn the ins and outs of being a gay or lesbian family.

4

⌒

SCHOOLS
DISCOVERING, OR CREATING,
OUR COMMON GROUND[1]

I am a first grade teacher. When I teach the family
unit in my classroom, I always send a letter home
telling the parents that ... we will ... also learn
about all kinds of alternative families, including
families with gay and lesbian parents.

—ALLAN ARNABOLDI[2]

From the early colonial days up to the latter part of the nineteenth century, most education took place in a rather ad hoc fashion. Children were either taught at home, especially in the rural
parts of this country, with a few books around like the Bible and
cross-point samplers that had the alphabet and numbers, or in
one-room schoolhouses, using *McGuffey's Second Reader*, with its
religious morality tales, and other books of virtues. Those who
were wealthy had tutors or attended private boarding schools

In the earliest part of the twentieth century, as the institution
known as "public schools" was taking off nationwide, the overriding
educational philosophy and cultural ethos were quite egalitarian

as well as rooted in economics. Public schools were a great boon to uniting this country, instilling in students a sense of American identity and pride. The hope was also that the schools would create an educated workforce as well as serve an integral role in blending all the children from various largely European nationalities into becoming, first and foremost, "American." In this "melting pot," the public schools quickly taught all the children English along with civic lessons on the public mores or ethics of this country.

However, early proponents of the public school system, like John Dewey and Horace Mann, probably never considered that the public schools would not only teach children (and their families) to be American, but would also teach children and teenagers stereotypical male and female roles and promote heterosexuality. In one sense, public schools promote the culturally blessed status quo of the surrounding society; at the same time, the schools themselves establish what will be the surrounding culture's status quo, all in the name of promoting the common good.[3]

In reflecting upon my experience in public schools, as well as the experience that my children have had in public schools of the twenty-first century, there is still gender-set role modeling that goes on daily. For example, many high schools still have homecoming and spring prom kings and queens, and there are the men's teams and the women's teams, even though women's teams have made great strides in the last few decades, thanks to federal laws. Among elective course work, except for courses that are mandatory for all students, male and female alike, many of the classes have explicit gender designations—for example, women's chorale versus men's chorale—and unwritten gender agendas. Mostly male students attend car mechanic and wood shop classes, while sewing classes have primarily female students. And I was surprised at my son Parker's recent graduation when most of the academic honors went not to the boys or to a healthy balance of boys and girls, but primarily to the girls in his graduating class of eighth graders. As Parker has said to me many times, "Dad, it just isn't cool to be smart *and* a guy in middle school!"

Beyond gender roles and expectations, there is also the issue of how the norm of heterosexuality is standardized in the context of the public schools. For example, when gays and lesbians have tried to "mix things up" in terms of gender-specific roles, like who can bring a date to a high school prom (the norm being that only boys and girls can date one another), there has been public consternation when two gay young men or two lesbian young girls bring each other to a prom.[4] Public consternation only becomes heightened—or tweaked—when the homecoming queen is a gay young man, or the homecoming king is a lesbian young woman. Some young people are brave enough to challenge the sexual role model "status quo."

But school is more than the academic classes. As my former wife Pam, who teaches fifth grade in a public school, reminds me. She is a teacher, nurse, therapist, academically gifted teacher, special education teacher, gym teacher, musician, actor, marriage counselor, English-as-a-second-language teacher, administrator, sex educator, and recess supervisor, as well as a disciplinarian during lunch. Students bring with them not only their academic lives, but their entire lives to school, including issues at home as well as their personal growth issues. We know that teachers play various roles and perform many functions; they also set the "tone"; more specifically for this discussion, they provide (or withhold) an atmosphere of inclusiveness in a school. In other words, a school's teachers and administrators, along with its students, can either make their school a place that is inclusive of gay and lesbian students and of students whose parents are gay or lesbian, or it can be a place that is perhaps lukewarm to the presence of a child from a gay- or lesbian-headed household. Or it can be downright cold. It is a lesson that my family has learned the hard way.

BRINGING LIFE TO SCHOOL: "SOMETHING IS THE MATTER AT HOME!"

While I knew I was gay when I was in junior high and high school, I never wanted it to be known publicly. I hid as well as I could, dating various girls throughout six years of school; joining the track team in junior high school; running for school offices (and winning); and blending in with the other students fashion-wise, even though I had an opportunity to model clothes in high school.

However, my children experienced my being "outed" as a gay dad by several teachers in the same middle school in Chapel Hill, North Carolina. I remember two distinct events in each of my children's lives in which having a gay dad was recognized as "unique" in my children's educational careers. The first time was with Adrianne. At the time, she was in sixth grade, which in the Chapel Hill–Carrboro Community School District meant that she was in her first year in middle school. I had moved out of the home that I shared with the children and their mom in January 1999. I was living in a condominium nearby and preparing to go on a sabbatical leave in Minnesota for the upcoming spring semester of 2000.

Adrianne had hit a rough patch in middle-school classes, and we were called by her team of teachers to talk with her about her progress in classes, or lack thereof. I distinctly remember that we talked about "changes in the home," which may have caused some of Adrianne's lack of attention to the issues at hand in her classes. Somehow in the conversation, the issue that I had moved out of the house where I lived with their mother because I was gay became an "aha" moment for one of the teachers. From that meeting, the word spread, far and wide, that Adrianne has a gay dad.

Not only did the personal information circulate that year among Adrianne's teachers, it was passed down to the next generation.

Four years later, when Parker hit a rough patch in an English class because (he said) he did not like the teacher, I sat down with the teacher to talk about his class behavior. Without any prompting from me, the teacher said, "We all know about the special circumstances of Parker's family." "What 'special circumstances'?" I asked. "Well, we know *why* you and Parker's mother separated and divorced." "Really?" I said, and dropped the subject there.

Old but good stories die hard.

❧

Having a gay dad or lesbian mom is a title or sign that will attach itself to our children without our permission. Though there is no symbol or sign that says THIS CHILD'S PARENT IS STRAIGHT, there seems to be a symbol or sign that says THIS CHILD'S PARENT IS GAY/ LESBIAN, like there is a stigma in having a gay or lesbian parent. It is something that we have to help our children become accustomed to, and we need to empower them to respond or react in a healthy manner, while we parents "destigmatize" being gay or lesbian.

In conversations with both of my children, I have discovered the techniques they have used in dealing with "the sign." Parker describes some of his school friends who are not open or welcoming of people who are gay or lesbian in the following way: "They're kind of blind to what they can't see. What they can't see is that being gay isn't really a bad thing. Being gay isn't something you choose; it's who you are."

Parker has defended me before in various places, explaining to others why it is cool to have a gay dad. For example, he had to explain to one of the assistants in an after-school program he used to attend that his dad is gay. When the assistant was miffed and said to Parker, "No, he's not; no way," Parker turned to another assistant, who corrected his colleague, saying, "Yeah, his dad's gay ... so what of it?" End of discussion.

This is not something I had deal with when I was Parker's age. When first hearing this story, it both pained me to hear what Parker faced, and yet I was I was proud of Parker's ability to live honestly in a world that covets lies regarding sexual orientation.

As for Adrianne, her group of friends and associates do not understand the downside of being gay. Attending a church with many lesbian or gay couples, as well as growing up in a family in which many of our friends are gay or lesbian, the issue of being a child of a gay parent has lost some of its novelty as well as some of its drawbacks or fears.

When I asked her what it's like to have a "gay parent," she thought a few seconds and simply said, "I can't imagine life being any other way." She explained it this way: "Sometimes telling friends about my dad's partner, some of my friends don't get it, but when I explain it, that my Dad is gay and has a partner, they get it."

When I asked her if it's strange, having a Dad who is gay, she says it was at first. She was around seven years old when I more or less "came out" to her and Parker. But after a while, there was really nothing extraordinarily different: "Now it's just kind of who I am. This is how life is right now. I accept it."

Adrianne continues:

"I think in general it's cool. There aren't a whole lot of people who have gay parents that I know, so in a lot of respects, I feel kind of unique in that kind of way because there are so few people who have gay parents that I come in contact with, that I feel unique in that respect.

"It's kind of irritating when there are so many homophobic people that I see on a regular basis, and will say 'Oh, that's so gay!' That's really irritating. For me, you're gay, and you never know who hears that, and you don't know how they're going to hear it, and being in the closet, they may not want to come out even more.

"I've never been made fun of because I have a gay dad. People look at me weird, kind of with curiosity, what it's like to have a gay dad. It's come to be a very normal thing. It's come to be the way things are. I like it."

GRADUATION TIME

Earlier, I wrote about Parker's graduation from middle school, in which he deftly explained our family unit to his friends, addressing Dean, my partner, as his step-dad. I'm not sure how awkward Parker felt about doing this, knowing that he and Adrianne have come to understand Dean as a step-dad in every sense of the word except for the legal title, which he cannot have because of the laws in our state.

One of the most beautiful moments in watching my daughter introduce her now-blended family of origin was at her graduation from middle school, in which she introduced the entire family in this way to her teachers and friends: "This is my mom, this is my dad, this is my dad's partner, and this is my little brother." She said it to one and all, without missing a beat. She had nothing to hide. Even though we had not discussed what to do in this situation, she seemed to know exactly what she was going to say.

Zoom ahead to a day in high school. Adrianne was waiting for me to pick her up, and she was standing with a group of three girlfriends. They were all laughing and giggling and peering into the car I was driving. I asked Adrianne what they were looking at, and she smiled and simply said, "I told them that you were gay, and they thought that was cool. They just wanted to see you in person." Most of her high school friends know Dean, my partner, or know *of* Dean, and she has told many of them that we go shopping, to shows, and to dinner together.

In the mazelike, bewildering hallways of our local public schools, with teachers, friends, other students, and administrators, all with their own biases and quirky families, my children seem to have figured out how to survive and thrive while living between two households, that of my former wife and that of two gay dads. And while I would love to play "Lord Protector" and dash anyone who questions them in life, that they are learning to explain who they are and who we are in their own way, in their own time, is about as good as it gets.

STRATEGIES FOR INCLUSION OF OUR CHILDREN ... AND OF US AS PARENTS

Some strategies that worked for us will make life not only in the public schools but in any school not only tolerable, but enjoyable.

- *Parent as educator:* In talking with a lesbian mom who had a son going into a private preschool program in "liberal" Chapel Hill, North Carolina, one of the stumbling blocks that the mother faced were teachers who were more uncomfortable in having to deal with the mothers being lesbians than with their son. The mother recounted how the teacher would always introduce her or her partner as the son's "lesbian moms," but that the same teacher would never refer to any of the other moms as the "straight moms." Finally, one of the "lesbian moms" had to point out to the one teacher the interesting discrepancy that was occurring in the simple act of introducing her to other parents. Soon after, the teacher no longer introduced the moms as "the lesbian moms."

  The bias, the prejudice that we face as gays and lesbians in some parts of our jobs or places where we like to hang out often continues or is carried over into most arenas of common life, like among preschool teachers, as well as teachers and administrators in elementary schools, middle schools, and high schools. We probably should not be surprised, but be ready to educate teachers, staff, and administrators alike, both for our sake, as well as for the sake of our children.

- *Gay-Straight Alliance (GSA):* In the 1990s, Gay-Straight Alliance groups sprang up in high schools and colleges around the country, offering a safe and supportive environment for lesbian, gay, straight allies, bisexuals, and transgendered youth. A common misunderstanding of the group is that it is a "hangout" for the LGBT students or a pick-up place for LGBT youth. The composition of the group differs depending on the year and the school, with some groups having primarily gay or lesbian students, while others have primarily straight allies. Some schools have tried to take away any stigma related to GSA with other titles, like "Rainbow Alliance" or "Spectrum."

  One of the helpful aspects of GSA groups in high schools and colleges is that they help educate others in a school context, honoring special days in the gay and lesbian community. For example, some GSA groups sponsor a "Day of Silence" in high schools, colleges, and middle schools, in which the participants do not speak all day, honoring the voice of those who are LGBT whose voices are not heard.

  Adrianne had an opportunity to be part of the Gay-Straight Alliance at Chapel Hill High School. She attended it when it was a positive experience for her—the members included gay, lesbian, and straight students—but left when there were more gay young men and no straight or lesbian young women. However, it was through her public participation in the group that some students learned that she was a safe ally for them, especially with a gay dad. Adrianne told me about one young woman whose mother had just come out to her daughter as a lesbian, but the daughter had no one else to talk to. Feeling alone and frantic, the young daughter poured out her heart to Adrianne on a school bus ride one morning because the young girl knew that I was gay. Adrianne befriended her when she needed a friend who understood.

- *Safe Zone Training:* Like GSA groups, since the 1990s, Safe Zone Training has emerged in high schools and colleges. Over a period of three or four sessions, trained and educated teachers provide other faculty, staff, and administrators of high schools and colleges information, education, and counseling services regarding issues facing LGBTS[5] students and other school members that would make them and their offices a "safe place" to come to when life in certain schools, departments, programs, or hallways became threatening or hostile. At the end of the training, the now-certified faculty, staff, or administrator display a sign or designation on their door, publicly stating that they have been trained to be a safe place for an LGBT or straight ally to come to in the school.

    I went through the program at Duke University. It could be strengthened by including training on helping straight allies, like my daughter and son. Sometimes, high school and college faculty members voice views that LGBTS students find hostile, and the students may find themselves threatened in terms of being in such learning environments. GSA and Safe Zone programs provide support in places.

- *Sex education and family units:* In North Carolina, as is true in other parts of the States, there is great debate about sex education. For the past few years, there has been a discussion on the role and place of condoms, abstinence-only programs, and whether or not homosexuality should be taught at all in the curriculum. The book *Love Makes a Family* includes the story of Allen Arnaboldi, a gay man who is also a father and a first-grade teacher. This is what he did with the sex curriculum he was handed, and how he amended it to include his family:

When I teach the family unit in my classroom, I always send a letter home telling the parents that in addition to the traditional nuclear family we will also learn about all kinds of alternative families, including families with gay and lesbian parents. Over the years, a few parents have expressed concerns because homosexuality was counter to their beliefs. I have said to them, "There are children in my class who have families with gay or lesbian members, and they need to know that our classroom is a safe place for them to be. We are talking about families, not about sex." After this explanation, these parents were fine.[6]

As I have written earlier in this book, as gay and lesbian parents, we are in the unenviable position of constantly being educators to help our children.

• *Do unto others: living by the Golden Rule:* Every school or classroom has a motto or pledge that encapsulates the ethos of the school. These are often rules of common courtesy that the school faculty, administrators, and students are asked to live by. One of the sayings that often appears is this: "We are to love one another as we have been loved, or want to be loved." It is a "Golden Rule" that we in America often fail to practice.

I remember when Adrianne was much younger, in elementary school, if I remember exactly, and she heard a reading from John 13:34 in which Jesus gives us a new commandment, "that you love one another. Just as I have loved you, you also should love one another." Adrianne was quite animated, tugging at my shirtsleeve and saying, "I didn't know Jesus knew my teacher! That's *her* saying!"

Carrying the practice of these words of Jesus into our public schools will let others know that we, as Christians, are not only people of love, but that we are Christ's disciples, by the love that we have for one another (John 13:34, 35). As gay and lesbian parents, we may need to help not only *our* children to live by these words, but enable others who espouse the Golden Rule to listen carefully and, if they so desire, to live carefully by these words in welcoming and including one and all—in the schools, the market, the church, or at home.

- *Challenge the status quo:* The presence of gays and lesbians in the workforce of teachers, administrators, and staff, along with students who are LGBT and parents, grandparents, aunts, uncles, and distant relatives, will invariably shake up the status quo. By our very public presence, we challenge the status quo of American education, which is, of course, populated by more heterosexuals than homosexuals. That's okay. What matters is that we learn the greater lesson of creating safe places in schools so that the gifts and talents of the next generation will build upon the successes and fix the failures of our generation. The hope is that, someday soon, we will arrive at a time of great inclusiveness, in which gay and straight will be able to learn, play, sing, act, perform great athletic feats, with no one worried about being gay, lesbian, or straight. Some of these lessons can begin right in our very own households, the subject of the next chapter.

5

❧

HOUSEHOLDS

TAKE ONE HETEROSEXUAL MOM, ADD TWO GAY DADS + TWO CHILDREN + TWO DOGS + ONE CAT = VERY FULL HOUSE

> Kids with gay parents—just like kids with mixed-race parents, divorced parents, disabled parents, turban-wearing parents, etc.—one day realize that their families are different, and that realization can be traumatic. And that, as they say, is okay.
>
> —DAN SAVAGE[1]

ADDING ASSAULT TO INSULT

Let me be clear about an earlier point: first, two gay men or two lesbian women can be a family. Period.

Second, gay or lesbian couples can make great parents, creating and tending to nurturing, loving, fun, stressed-filled, slightly neurotic, competitive households, just like any straight couple.

No matter what they say on the playgrounds in the cities and suburbs or wherever we take our children to play with other children of heterosexual couples, as gay and lesbian couples, *we can be parents and thus a larger family*. Some gay and lesbian households may choose to add a menagerie of dogs, cats, ferrets, fish, turtles, rabbits, rats (don't ask), snakes (been there, too), and a de-skunked skunk (once, and once only), along with the ranch home, two-car garage, and other amenities that follow the American script of being a family. But two gay men or two lesbian women begin the move toward being a family from the time they move in together and claim each other as a significant part, or partner, of life.

Critics assault us for taking the next step, for doing what is the *real* defining moment of being a family or household in America: when we add children to the coupled relationship. Many young married couples suffer the same assault: When is the baby coming? And after the first baby comes, the next question is, When's the next baby coming? After all, you don't want the child to be an *only* child?

In the real world, being and becoming a family—whether as a couple alone, or with pets, or with children—does not happen spontaneously. Somewhere along the line, there has to be a sense of intentionality and meaningfulness. Again, because we are not given the privilege of marriage or same-sex civil unions per se, it is hard to tell or give ourselves a "starting date" to say when we committed ourselves to being a couple or a family. Many friends of mine simply moved in together, and before they knew it, the years had passed by and they were, for all sense and purposes, a couple. We call such a heterosexual couple "common-law husband and wife," but there is no such legal designation for gays and lesbians.

Announcing to friends, family, and the world that "we're a couple" and thus "we're a family" is one thing, but we are also *always* in the process of *becoming* a family, *becoming* a household, *becoming* partners in a deeper, more meaningful way. Being and becoming a family is similar to the move from being *in* a house, apartment, townhouse, or condominium, to *being* and *becoming* a home, and thus being a family. In other words, being a family is a continual process of change and growth. Sometimes it will be great fun, and at other times a tough challenge.

Unfortunately, we experience this spoken or unspoken but implied comment from many heterosexual Americans: "Any child that grows up in a gay- or lesbian-headed household will turn out gay or lesbian, because of the parents influence."

The following statistics disprove the statement:

- Ninety-eight percent of the gays and lesbians in America were raised in heterosexual family units, and their heterosexuality did not seem to rub off;[2]

- There are over fourteen million members of lesbian and gay families in the United States, with the majority of the children being raised by lesbians.[3]

- One in six gay men have fathered or adopted a child, and more than one in three lesbians have given birth and/or adopted a child;[4]

- Over two million LGBT people are interested in adopting;[5]

- An estimated 65,000 adopted children are living with a lesbian or gay parent; 14,100 foster children are living with lesbian or gay parents;[6]

- Gay and lesbian parents are raising 4 percent of all adopted children in the U.S.[7]

Being gay or lesbian does not "rub off" on our children. But being human *does* rub off on children. Because we are human, we who are gay or lesbian desire as much as heterosexuals to be moms and dads, not only biologically, but also through adoption and foster programs. Not only are we adopting and taking in more foster children, but we are adopting and being foster parents to the very children that many heterosexuals do not desire.

The challenge before us, as gay and lesbian parents, is to feel "at home" in our own skins—sexually, emotionally, intellectually, spiritually, and physically—while also enabling our children to feel "at home" in theirs, as children of lesbian and gay couples. While we, as gays and lesbians, may have learned lessons of deceit, impersonating straight people and hiding our appearance in this world, oftentimes our children will feel the need to do the very same thing. They will try to hide us as parents. They will do impersonations, making other children feel that we're just like any straight family. And they will try to hide us, not only as parents (all children want to disown a parent from time to time), but as a gays or lesbians.[8]

In this chapter, first I want to discuss that we gay and lesbian parents who are raising children—and oftentimes grandchildren— in our homes are not only capable of raising children, but are quite good at it. Second, I want to show that "gay coupling" and raising children is not only a variable in the human condition, but of the entire animal kingdom, including penguins and flamingos. Last, I'll provide suggestions regarding how and where we can find support for our families, both locally, statewide, and nationally, and both out of and in the Church.

THE PROOF IS IN THE STUDIES AND LIFE

SOCIAL SCIENCE STUDIES

One of the criticisms toward gay and lesbian families is that we do not necessarily "make good parents," and thus are incapable of creating "good, nurturing households" for our children simply because we are gay or lesbian. This goes back to the erroneous argument raised by Jonathan Rauch: "To have kids = not being gay" because gays and lesbians do not have children because of the way we express our physical love does not lead to pro-creation … necessarily.[9]

The argument that some people have tried to make is that gay and lesbian couples have no need to be married because we do not raise children and, second, that we harm children by raising them. This argument has been refuted by solid social science research along with qualitative anecdotal research proving that gays and lesbians make fine parents. Brad Sears, who is executive director of the UCLA School of Law Williams Project on Sexual Orientation Law and Public Policy, and Alan Hirsch, a senior consultant for the project, wrote an article entitled "Straight Out Truth on Gay Parenting," which debunks the two claims made above.

The American Academy of Pediatrics' Committee on Psychosocial Aspects of Child and Family Health issued a report in 2002, the most recent comprehensive review of gay-parenting studies. It found no meaningful differences between children raised by gay parents and those raised by heterosexual parents.

The committee reviewed scientific literature encompassing three broad sets of studies. The first set assessed the attitudes, behavior and adjustments of lesbian and gay parents and found, according to the AAP report, "more similarities than differences in the parenting styles and attitudes of gay and non-gay fathers." Likewise, the research showed that lesbian mothers scored the same as heterosexual mothers in "self-esteem, psychological adjustment and attitudes toward child rearing."

The second set of studies looked at the gender identity and sexual orientation of children raised by gay parents. The committee report found that none of the several hundred children studied evinced gender identity confusion, wished to be of the other sex or consistently engaged in cross-gender behavior. No differences were found in the toy, game, activity, dress or friendship preferences of boys or girls with gay parents compared with those with heterosexual parents, nor any differences in sexual attraction or self-identification as gay.

The third research area discussed in the report covers children's emotional and social development. These studies have primarily compared children raised by lesbians who are divorced with children of divorced heterosexual mothers. No differences have been found in personality measures, peer group relationships, self-esteem, behavioral difficulties, academic success and quality of family relationships. The studies suggest only one meaningful difference: Children of lesbian parents are "more tolerant of diversity and more nurturing toward younger children than children whose parents are heterosexual."

The American Academy of Pediatrics report is the most prestigious of its kind, but it is not the only one. Most reviews of the social science research reach the same conclusion: The proposition that children suffer when raised by gay or lesbian parents is without basis. Indeed, some evidence suggests that the only significant difference between children raised by same-sex couples and children raised by heterosexual couples is that the former feel freer to explore occupations and behaviors unhampered by traditional gender roles—a good thing, perhaps.[10]

This report and several like it, along with anecdotal evidence, which is usually countered by some who are outwardly opposed to not only gay and lesbian parenting but to the idea of us being in long-term relationships, add to the evidence that being a child of gay or lesbian parents could be pretty good, both for the child as well as for the parents.

Or consider this recent article from CNN online by Taylor Gandossy:

"There is no credible social science evidence to support that gay parenting—and by extension, gay adoptive parenting—negatively affects the well-being of children," said Adam Pertman, executive director of the Evan B. Donaldson Adoption Institute. "It's quite clear that children do fine in homes led by gays and lesbians. That's a pretty basic bottom line." Pertman says his organization is not particularly involved in gay and lesbian issues—they support gay and lesbian parenting because it "serves children's interests." Several organizations—the National Adoption Center, the American Medical Association, American Psychological Association, the American Academy of Pediatrics—also say that having gay and lesbian parents does not negatively affect children.[11]

Why are our homes possibly "above average" in terms of the "quotient" or idea of care and compassion? This is a hunch: it may be because we have had to become more inventive, creative, and intentional about raising our children in a world of people who are often hostile to us, not because of anything we have done, but because of who we are: gays and lesbians.

For example, first because we have been denied the chance to share or to be expressive in our love in public, we are more likely to express our love more readily in our homes. Because our children grow up in homes in which women and men can find love with each other, as well as love for our children, our children may be exposed to more ways of being loved in this world than many of their friends who grow up in heterosexual households. My children both know that two heterosexual people can love one another, as can two gay men, and that both ways of being in relationship are good and right ways to be in relationship.

Second, because of our "minority status" in this country and because we are continually defending ourselves and how we live and love, we have to become more psychologically savvy in communicating and being in touch with our feelings. So our relationships may be more intense, intellectual and spiritual, than those of other couples. Almost by necessity, we must continually communicate our wants, our needs, and our feelings. It is not that gay and lesbian couples are more sensitive than straight couples, but we are forced, by some of the politics of the church as well as of the state, to talk to each other about what is going on in our lives.

Last, we who are gay and lesbian are aware of politics, especially regarding how we fit in or do not fit into the American idea of family. Thus, we try to be the best families on the block because we know we are under a magnifying glass. For example, while I have no doubts that my parents support the way I parent, I know that they would have liked it if I had come out later in life, after the children were out of high school. They know that the children would face some of the hate-filled speech directed primarily at me as a gay man.

ANIMAL STUDIES: PENGUINS, FLAMINGOS, AND KOALA BEARS, OH MY!

What has been interesting in recent years is that we have learned that gay and lesbian parenting is not limited to human beings. To quote Cole Porter, "Birds do it, bees do it." As we watch members of the animal kingdom live out their lives, drawing conclusions about our own habits and ways of life from reflecting on the lives of animals, we have learned some interesting things. For example, Duke University's phenomenal lemur center, in which the habitual lives of lemurs have been studied exhaustively, provide insights into how human beings relate to each other.

The "naturalness" of being a gay or lesbian parent was recently uncovered in animal studies; in addition, same-sex pairing of animals seems rather, well, ordinary. Consider the stories of penguins, flamingos, and koalas. The most familiar and now famous story of two male penguins who are in a monogamous same-sex relationship in New York City's Central Park Zoo. People started to recognize that there was something unique going on between two penguins, Roy and Silo. Rob Gramzy, their zookeeper, noticed that the two not only had a "thing" for each other, but showed great parenting skills with a penguin egg.

Roy and Silo's behavior indicated that they really wanted a kid. Zookeepers gave them a dummy penguin egg to see if they'd actually incubate it. When they did, zookeepers gave them an actual egg, which Roy and Silo again incubated. When the baby chick was born, Roy and Silo cared for it, feeding it yummy regurgitated smelt and keeping it warm until it could survive on its own.

> Years later, Roy and Silo are still going strong. And so are all their heterosexual penguin pals who share the tank with them. So that dispels one myth about gay marriage: Roy and Silo's commitment to each other has not destroyed the sanctity of the other penguin marriages. Gramzy said the penguin divorce rate remains the same as it was before Roy and Silo hooked up.[12]

Likewise, there is the story from a wildlife refuge in Britain in which two flamingos, Carlos and Ferdinand, become "foster parents" to a young chick who was abandoned by its mother when it was still just an egg. Carlos and Ferdinand followed all the habits that other maternal and paternal flamingos would follow in caring for an egg and then nurturing their foster child. Carlos and Ferdinand had been together for six years and had stolen eggs before from other nests, so the wildlife refuge people had little doubt that the flamingos could pull it off.

Along with gay couplings, there is the Australian study of female koala bears who have found other females to mate with, leading scientists to conclude there is lesbian attraction among female koalas: "In a study of one hundred and thirty koalas, scientists from the University of Queensland (in Brisbane, Australia, found that some females rejected advances by males and then were willing participants with females moments later. Some of the koalas' 'sex sessions' involved up to five other female koalas at a time."[13]

These few examples of other animal behaviors suggest that a lesbian or gay couple (animal or human) can be just as adept—or inept—as any heterosexual couple.

OUR NURTURING HOMES

In this generation, we will always be known as "the gay couple" or "the lesbian couple" who are raising children, and our children will be known by other people—friends and family members alike—as children of gay or lesbian parents. While others do not call themselves "heterosexual" or "straight" couples, since we are in the minority, we continue bear the signifier of "the gay/lesbian family."

So what can we do to make our homes nurturing places in light of being "out" to others in modern society? Consider the following list of comments, thoughts, and activities:

- *Let love rule.* Whether we have a family with children via adoption, natural means, foster children, or some other kind of arrangement, as has been true with every family system throughout time in all cultures, love is the necessary common denominator that keeps us together and thriving as a family. An essay in CNN online told the story of Jackson Manford-Roach, who is five years old and was born in Guatemala, and his dads, Jeffrey Roach and Ken Manford, along with a similar story with Rob and Clay Calhoun, all living in Georgia. When asked what holds the family together and what makes this group a family, Rob Calhoun simply said, "We're not moms, we're not heterosexual. We're not biological parents." But "we're totally equal and just as loving as female parents, as straight parents, and biological parents. Love makes a family, not biology or gender."

  While love *sounds* good for making and holding a family together, what *is* love? The writer Frederick Buechner wrote this wonderful description of love, which he sees as a rare combination of *philia*, *agape*, and *eros*:

  > The unabashed *eros* of lovers, the sympathetic *philia* of friends, *agape* giving itself away freely no less for the murderer than for his victim—these are all varied

manifestations of a single reality. To lose yourself in another's arms, or in another's company, or in suffering for all who suffer, including the ones who inflict suffering upon you—to love yourself in such ways is to find yourself.[14]

And on top of this, there are as many ways to love and be in loving relationships as there are people in this world. How love is expressed in one family—with big bear hugs and loud expressions of "I love you"—may be different in another family, in which love is shown in the daily tasks one does around a household, and soft words of love in a prayer at night. What matters is not *how* love is shared in a family necessarily, but *that* love is shared in a family.

- *Family name.* In my first and only marriage, my former wife Pam took my last or family name, "Mitchell." It was three or four years later, after reading a lot of feminist theology, that we hyphenated our name to "Webb-Mitchell." Upon our divorce, Pam took back her "maiden" name. After the children, who were "Webb-Mitchell," told me that they did not want to be the only ones in the world with that name, I decided not to go back to my "maiden" name, Mitchell.

  Some gay and lesbian families, to express their solidarity and togetherness, take on each other's names, creating a hyphenated last name and giving this name to the child or children. Still other lesbian and gay families take on one person's last names, giving this name to the children as well. And still others hold onto their last names and distribute the name among the children if they have two or more children. Finally, some families look at the whole experience as doing something new and change all of their last names, which undoubtedly will confuse genealogists in the future.

- *Being a parent*: learn to be an authority and authoritative, not authoritarian. I have found that especially when our children are younger, we may need to step in and explain our "unique" family to others—in public school classrooms, churches, social gatherings, neighborhood meetings, and playgrounds—and act as an authority on gay- or lesbian-headed households. While there is no truth in the claim that all gay or all lesbian couples and families look and act the same or that we are somehow a homogeneous community speaking with one voice, we will often have an opportunity to share with others outside our family circle our life stories and what works in our families. Reluctant though we may be to share such private matters, stepping up to the plate as someone who possesses authoritative experience about being part of a gay couple with children and speaking out when injustice is in the air is praiseworthy.

Stepping up also works inside the family system. One or both parents need to be authorities, but not bully authoritarians. Major decisions should be made after getting input from all family members. Once a decision is rendered by the parent or parents, they have to stick with them. Weekly "family council" meetings are not a bad idea and help in making good decisions within the family. At these meetings, issues and activities of the family are discussed and, if need be, voted on or concensus reached when a decision is to be made.

- *Share responsibilities and accountabilities.* While love may hold a family together, all members of the household must share the responsibilities and be accountable to one another ... with love, of course.

That this could be your opportunity to demonstrate that old-fashioned gender roles and job descriptions do not fit together as they did in the homes that we grew up in. In some cases, men cook the meals, wash the clothes, and clean toilets, while women are great at woodworking, gardening (including mowing the lawn and edging), as well as fixing cars. This is a chance for us to change the script and to make our family in our own image.

- *Create family times and rituals.* One way to help affirm the family we are and are becoming is through new family traditions, celebrating our lives by borrowing rituals and celebrations from churches or synagogues, as well as celebrating cultural traditions such as Memorial Day, Mothers' Day, and so on. These celebrations encourage us to think about who we are and what we are becoming as a family as we celebrate the old and rejoice in the new.[15]

Because in many of our families all the members are "chosen"—like a family consisting of a gay or lesbian couple, who chose each other, along with children who may be adopted or foster children, also chosen—a unique set of celebrations could honor when each person came into the family circle. For example, some families in which children were adopted from foreign countries celebrate the day the children were selected or picked up and they were given their new names; they call it "Naming Day."

There can also be anniversary parties, celebrating not only a couple's anniversary together, but when the family came altogether as a family. It is important to affirm and reaffirm that "something new" is happening here as we create new "branches" on our family trees of origin.

More gay and lesbian couples are putting their "wedding" or "same-sex civil union" announcements in Sunday papers such as the *New York Times*. In the same section of the newspaper, families put in photos of couples celebrating twenty-five- and fifty-year anniversaries. There is no reason why we could not submit such announcements and celebrations in local and national publications, telling the world that we exist and are thriving in American society.

WE ARE PIONEERS, WRITING THE FIRST DRAFT OF THIS STORY

Our children live both with their mother, who lives in the same town where we live, and in our household. There is a fairly good chance that many people who are reading this book are in the throes of "writing" or "creating" their families as gay and lesbian.

But we are not working from a blank slate. We were born into families, and we will more than likely borrow some of the "tricks of the trade" of raising a family from our families of origin. While some of the gender-specific stereotypes may be guiding us in terms of jobs around the house, and our way of disciplining children or relating parent-to-parent may take on the tone and words of our own parents, we need to remember, at least once a day, that no one has ever done "our way" for being family before.

For example, my partner's way of being a parent—being a true Southerner—is slightly different than my thoroughly northern or Yankee way of being a parent. Sometimes our styles mesh and click, and sometimes we butt heads. What makes it even more interesting is that being two white, all-American males in relationship *also* has its own dynamic, and throw in my son's habits and ways, being raised as an all-American male (we call ourselves "two gay men and a straightie" after the TV show *Two and a Half Men*), and the chest thumping, "my way or the highway" bravado gets going. It is unlike anything my partner or I grew up in. But the exciting part is remembering that we're the first generation to map out this way of living together. Then we can be as creative, silly, and frustrated as we want to be.

"WHEN WE GET OLDER, LOSING OUR HAIR, MANY YEARS FROM NOW"—WE MAY BE GRANDPARENTS

In one of his earlier movies, *The Sum of Us*, Russell Crowe plays a gay character. In the movie, he remembers his mother's lesbian relationship and that he had two great aunts who were lesbians. This being "gay" or "lesbian" may run in the family. The closet doors in this movie, among several generations, in many homes, open wide and wider each time the tale is told.

Most gay and lesbian people, knowing that who we are is more than likely genetic in origin, wonder at times who else was gay or lesbian in our families. We may recall the comments and behaviors of long-gone relatives who could not live out in the open, given that far fewer gays or lesbians were "out" in public.

Nowadays, there are more lesbian and gay couples who are not only parents but also are grandparents. Their sons and daughters—who may or may not be gay or lesbian—are having children, and the next generation of "out" gay and lesbian couples have already begun. Along with retirement villages for gay and lesbian couples, grandparenthood is right around the corner for many readers of this book.

NETWORKING

Organizations are sprouting around the country that are trying to meet the needs of gay- and lesbian-headed households. Groups like COLAGE (Children of Lesbians and Gays Everywhere) and GLPCI (Gay and Lesbian Parenting Coalition, International), have existed for some time. There are more websites, booths offering opportunities to network at Pride parades and festivals, and parenting workshops in churches and other social clubs. An increasing number of blogs address both lesbian moms and gay dads.

Likewise, vacation and social opportunities are more available. For example, Rosie and Kelly O'Donnell now host cruises for families like ours with children, and COLAGE hosts a national gathering of families like ours in Provincetown, Massachusetts, every August. And picnics, cookouts, and other group activities for families like ours exist throughout this country. PFLAG also hosts opportunities nationwide for get-togethers. (For additional information, see the list of websites in appendix A on page 146.)

IT'S ALL IN THE FAMILY

In family therapy courses, in family therapy sessions in which I've been the therapist, and in family therapy sessions in which I was the client, I've learned that the dynamics of a family are more or less learned, passed on from one generation to the next. If the behaviors are learned, then they can be unlearned as well. We can learn new ways to function in our homes and elsewhere, as we try to make our households "sanctuaries," places of growth, and retreats from the crazy world in which we live.

I have also learned that we can be resilient in relationships. We can snap back, forgive one another, learn from our mistakes, and love one another with greater insight and acceptance each and every time we goof up.

While we are in the process of mapping out a new way to be a family, others are trying to do the very same thing. The more we share our stories, the more likely it is that other gay- and lesbian-headed households may avoid some of our mistakes and move on with grace toward being an extraordinary family.

In the next chapter, I will focus on creating the couple relationship, whether it is civil union or, preferably, a "marriage." While "marriage" may be claimed by religious communities as "their" word and practice, it really is a legal term in the United States.

6

MARRIAGE: THE NEXT FRONTIER

SAME-SEX MARRIAGE, CIVIL UNIONS ...
AND THE CHILDREN!

> Like interracial marriage and the national debate
> over race, same-sex marriage stands at the very heart
> of the issue of accepting homosexuality in America
> yet remains the most elusive prize of all.
>
> —ANDREW SULLIVAN[1]

Amid preparing and leading worship, celebrating Eucharist, bap-
tizing babies, visiting shut-ins, attending rallies for just causes,
leading Sunday school classes, writing newsletters, leading Session
meetings, cleaning up after large and small events, and rooting
for the basketball teams, one of a pastor's responsibilities is performing weddings. Having witnessed and been a best man and
groomsman in several weddings, as well as the groom, I perform
a pretty good wedding, if I say so myself. Or I did. Until I separated, divorced, and came out of the closet. Today, weddings
are not so easy for me to perform. Don't get me wrong: I give it
my all. I simply have a hard time going through the ritual now

because I cannot marry in my state of North Carolina. And there are legislators in the state of North Carolina who would like to create a constitutional amendment to be sure I never am able to marry in this state or in any other state.[2]

Let me explain: I live in sin. Many who read this book will be glad to know that I at least acknowledge it openly. It's not because I'm divorced. I am referring to my living with another man and having "conjugal relations" with him, outside the bounds of marriage, same-sex civil union, or any other name we could call this long-term relationship. In fact, the date that Dean and I celebrate as our anniversary is the first time we ever, truly, seriously "dated" each other. In fact, most LGBT couples celebrate their anniversaries on the date they first started dating or made love with one another. While married heterosexual couples mark their anniversaries on the date that the state acknowledged that they are married, we who are LGBT do not have this luxury.[3]

I stand up, before and in the presence of God, family members, friends, strangers, and congregants as the minister for the wedding, and my guts are churning with unease. As I explain the intent of marriage to the congregation, ask for the affirmation of family and friends for this marriage, read Scripture, preach a short sermon, read the vows, watch the swap of rings, lighting of candles, filling of sand jars, and then proclaim the couple husband and wife, I am filled with a mix of deep and dark emotions and confusing, paradoxical thoughts. I want the same rules applied to me and my partner, along with all the laws, privileges, and rights that this couple will now enjoy, especially the groom, who is marrying for the fourth time. He is in his twenties and secretly gay. I want the public affirmation and celebration, with all the showers and choosing of dinner plate options and a honeymoon on a faraway coast. I want the opportunity to have others know us openly as a couple, whatever that might mean. And I can have none of it.

The surprise and paradox: the man of God who has married over a hundred couples in twenty-five years is gay and cannot wed himself. The man who led the couple through the ups and downs of couple's counseling cannot wed himself. The man who just announced that these two are now husband and wife, before God and this company of witnesses, cannot wed. I've been told that I do weddings very well by many people. I do them well because I have researched them and their aftermath. I know about marriages with mysterious shadows. I know how some married couples have the ability to bounce back when thing get too awkward and I have seen when silence is more at home in the relationship than either the husband or the wife.

So what is it about marriage, same-sex unions, or committed relationships that so many of us who are LGBT want, crave, or desire? More specifically, what kind of impact would it have upon our lives as parents of children?

IT'S A WEDDING, A CIVIL UNION, A SAME-SEX MATING RITUAL, OR, WELL, WHAT IS "IT"?

If the 1960s was the public "coming out" in the Stonewall age of the gay community (June 27, 1969), then the 1990s was the decade of same-sex unions and marriages of gays and lesbians. With the passage of Vermont's bill allowing civil unions of gays and lesbians, signed by then-Governor Howard Dean, there was a sense of celebration among many gays and lesbians for this public affirmation of our relationships.

The definitions of same-sex civil union and same-sex marriage, however, need clarification. While many of us who are gays and lesbians want some way of honoring our relationship among family and friends, what we also desire are not only the benefits and protections of the state and federal government given to heterosexual couples, especially with children (read "tax break/credit"), but also recognition that we are actually couples. As Jonathan Rauch wrote so well, being a homosexual equaled not being able to be married. However, the opposite was also true: to be married meant that one wasn't gay or lesbian, and to have children in the marriage meant that one was really not gay or lesbian, because gays and lesbians cannot have children![4]

In 2003, the Supreme Court of the State of Massachusetts did what no other state had ever done—approved gay marriage.[5] As Jonathan Rauch wrote, "It was the shot heard around the world."[6] The court acknowledged that civil marriage is at once a personal commitment to another and a highly public celebration of ideals of mutuality, companionship, and family.[7] Suddenly, gay or lesbian same-sex unions and civil unions, in which we had many of the same or similar state protections and benefits of a heterosexual married couple, seemed to be "marriage-lite."[8] Furthermore, what many of us who are in gay and lesbian coupled relationships wanted was and is not a redefinition of marriage per se that would include us, but all the rights, benefits, and protections of the state and federal laws currently offered to heterosexual couples. For example, there are currently 1,138 ways in which married couples are accorded special status under federal law.[9]

Meanwhile, the battle lines had been drawn. In 1996, President Clinton signed on for the federal Defense of Marriage Act, DOMA, making it the law of the land that marriage is between one man and one woman. In the 2000 and 2004 federal and state election cycles, more states throughout the country amended their respective constitutions to prohibit gays and lesbians from marrying, with President Bush and many Republican senators pushing for a federal amendment to the U.S. Constitution making it impossible for lesbian and gay couples to be married.

While some states are pushing for more laws and benefits for gay and lesbian couples and other states are still trying to amend their constitutions prohibiting gays and lesbians from marrying, there is an additional push by some in the gay and lesbian community. Those of us who are Christians want not only state and federal protections, benefits, and laws; we want our respective denominations and churches to think through, theologically, what is marriage. We are offering the Church universal an opportunity to rethink, reimagine, reconfigure, and reaffirm the meaning of a wedding, a marriage, and a committed relationship in God's sight as well as in that of Christ's followers. Instead of simply filling in the blanks, changing the officiant's pronouncing "husband and wife" and to "husband and husband" or "wife and wife," here is an opportunity for religious communities to reconsider the theological basis of weddings and marriages.

However, our challenge to these institutions is not something new. Weddings and the institution of marriage are historically evolving concepts.

DEFINING MARRIAGE

Marriage, according to the dictionary is "the social institution under which a man and woman establish their decision to live as husband and wife by legal commitments, religious ceremonies, etc."[10] There are important parts of this description that make the debate about marriage volatile. For example, as a "social institution," the definition or description of what is marriage can change, depending on surrounding societal or group decisions about what is or is not marriage. The definition is not written in stone. Not one chapter or verse in the Old Testament or in the New provides a formula for how to perform a wedding or defines a marriage. While many of us clergy read from Genesis 2:24, "A man leaves his father and his mother and clings to his wife and they become one flesh," and from 1 Corinthians 13 about "love," there is nothing in Scripture that points to a recipe for success in marriage or long-term relationships. And while there is a wedding feast mentioned in chapter two of the Gospel of John, all we really know about the wedding is that Jesus performed his first miracle at it, according to the gospel writer. Lastly, the Apostle Paul made much ado about *not* getting married, believing that with Jesus Christ coming back any day now, people should be preparing for more important things than getting betrothed.

Whether we look at marriage through the lens or practices of the social, spiritual or religious, legal, or governmental aspects of the union,[11] there has been a great deal of change in the customs and mores of marriage throughout time, in all civilizations. The only unchanging aspect is that marriage seems to be between two people, and everything after that seems to be up for grabs.

THE BYGONE DAYS OF ARRANGED MARRIAGE

How have weddings and marriages changed? According to biblical scholars of the Old or the New Testament, as well as historians of other Middle Eastern and European cultures, many if not most marriages were arranged affairs, in which the betrothal of a man and woman was not decided by the love interests of the couple, but by their families. The reasons for arranged marriages, which existed up to and throughout the nineteenth and early twentieth centuries even in America (and still quietly practiced by some cultures in this country), are numerous. Some arranged marriages were for economic reasons, with the marrying together of two landlord families. Some arranged marriages united kingdoms or fiefdoms together, a theme that appears in many of Shakespeare's plays. Other relationships were arranged between two "good families," in which it was hoped that the good "genetic pool" of one family would be happily wed and bred with another good "pool" of genes. To this very day, there are "mail-order brides": couples do not necessarily "woo" each other before they meet, but a man simply looks online and "orders" a bride from another country. Marriages are still arranged in countries in the Middle East, in India, and in other countries and cultures around the world.

When people today talk about wanting a "biblical marriage," it is important to remember that most biblical marriages were mostly arranged affairs. For example, in the book of Ruth, after Ruth's husband (Naomi's son) dies, we understand that Ruth's marriage was an arranged relationship, in which feelings of love were secondary to the marriage that had been brokered by families. That is why Ruth's words are so eloquent: "Do not press me to leave you or to turn back from following you! Where you go, I will go; where you lodge, I will lodge; your people shall be my people, and your God my God" (Ruth 1:16).

Likewise, some biblical scholars strongly suggest that Jesus' mother, Mary, was in an arranged relationship with Joseph, her betrothed, as was the custom at that time, causing much debate as to whether Joseph *really* knew (in the biblical sense) Mary before he was religiously wed to her. More than likely, their relationship was an arranged affair, uniting two families together, and not based on a love interest between two young lovers, as the movies portray it.

THE CURRENT DAYS OF ROMANTIC LOVE-BASED MARRIAGES

Up to the nineteenth century, the arranged marriage was fairly common and ordinary; the woman became an object owned by the man, with the passing of a dowry and, if possible, property, titles, thrones, or a good serf in European society. But in the nineteenth century, along with the creation of the Valentine's Day card industry, both European and American cultures gravitated toward a romantic, love-based arrangement for marriage. While Romeo and Juliet were denied their love-based relationship because of family animosity and the family's right to arrange marriages, modern day couples can now choose whom they want to marry, based not on fealty to families, kingdom, civilizations, or economic pursuits, but on the human emotion of love.

This "love connection" has become the basis of today's weddings and marriages. Whether or not people are attracted to each other physically, emotionally, intellectually, financially, spiritually; because of social class, status, notoriety and fame (or infamy), or political power; or for some other unexplained reason that is not quite tangible ("charisma"), there is a degree of personal "choice" in the decision-making process.

In sum, marriage itself is a constantly changing, evolutionary term and concept and practice that is always in the process of being remade and reimagined in each and every culture, given the latest trends and cultural shifts. There is no such thing as a "traditional" wedding or a "traditional" marriage, just as there is no "traditional" family, because the traditions themselves keep changing and mutating. After all, weddings, marriages, and families are all culturally dependent terms and practices.

Given the heat of the discussions and the emotional uproar occurring in American society, which always accompanies any large social change, my hunch is that we are on the cusp of seeing, hearing, witnessing yet one more "turn of the wheel" of cultural evolution as more gay and lesbian couples choose to marry, and start families. Such change is good for society, for the Church, and for the family itself.

FOR THE GOOD OF SOCIETY: THE ARGUMENT FOR SAME-SEX MARRIAGE AND CIVIL UNIONS[12]

Why does society, the Church, and gay and lesbian couples and their families want or need marriage or same-sex civil unions?

- Socially, for gays and lesbians, marriage or same-sex civil unions provide an arrangement that fosters stability in their relationships. For some, the ad hoc nature of gay and lesbian relationships, in which we have nothing tying us to one another or helping to deepen a relationship so that it is able to make it over the hurdles of life, can get wearying. Commitment is like a "four-letter" word for some in our community.

- As heterosexuals know full well, while it can cost only a few dollars to get married, it can take hundreds of thousands of dollars to divorce. I have counseled many engaged couples, primarily heterosexual, about the ins and outs of relationships, hopefully opening their eyes, ears, hearts, and minds to a relationship's highs and lows. By thinking it through, talking it through, and processing it, many heterosexuals are given the opportunity to ponder and reflect what they are doing as they move into a closer relationship. What has amazed me and saddened me is that many gay and lesbian couples do not have or take the opportunity for such counseling before entering a relationship that both hope is long term.

- Marriage has a way of designating the "other" in our life as significant, as someone to whom we are committed and for whom we are responsible. In marriage, couples gain certain legal and social protections that make it easier for them to be known as a legally recognized couple and to live together. Jonathan Rauch is correct in understanding that marriage—unlike domestic partnerships or same-sex unions—gives gay and lesbian couples the mystique of social expectations that we, strangely enough, try to "live up to." In a real sense, married couples accept social responsibility for each other.[13]

For example, I already practice introducing myself with Dean as "Hi, I'm Brett, and this is my partner, Dean," which is how I used to introduce my former wife: "Hi, I'm Brett, and this is my wife, Pam." Having been in New Zealand and Australia, I prefer the designation "partner," which in those countries is used between husband and wife as well as for same-sex unions. Calling Dean "my husband" is as awkward as his calling me "husband." But these names and the freedom to name one another in this manner provide a sense of legitimacy that the state does not give us ... at this time.

FOR THE GOOD OF THE CHURCH: SAME-SEX MARRIAGE

In the United States, marriage is a civil, state contract. After all, there is a signing of a license, which is part and parcel of the act of marriage. It is weird to acknowledge that I am, in a sense, representing the State of North Carolina when I "legally wed" a man and woman who become husband and wife "by the laws of the state."

But there is something about a church wedding that brings together family and friends, in the presence of God and in the communion of saints, that I would like and am ready to fight for. After all, they were present at my first marriage, why not at this one to another man?

- Weddings and marriages are a reminder that we are not a couple by ourselves, but that we need the support of a community of others who believe what we believe, as they, in turn, need our support and encouragement. And not only do we, as adults need this affirmation—so do our children.

- At baptism, we are told that we are now a part of the community of Christian faith and are responsible to it. This includes weddings and marriages along with the well-being of our children. In baptism, we are promised that, regardless of whether we are LGBT or straight, we are part of Christ's body, made in the image of God, a truth that becomes part of who we are through and in the power of the Spirit.

- Think how much good it does for a child or young person to know and feel that his or her dads' or moms' relationship is "honored and recognized by all," instead of something that cannot be talked about behind backs or must be hidden. The acknowledgement of a relationship in a community of faith makes it known that the family unit itself is valued and affirmed as part of the community of faith.

Of course, the possibility of having a wedding and marriage honored by a church would mean that being gay or lesbian is no longer considered a "lifestyle choice," but an affirmation of who and whose we are as parts of God's good creation; and that being gay or lesbian in today's world is a good in the view of the Holy Trinity and the Church. In the end, what we are asking for is to make gay and lesbian sex and love as noble and dignified as straight sex and love.[14]

FOR THE GOOD OF THE FAMILY:
CHILDREN AND SAME-SEX MARRIAGE

What marriage brings for the good of the family is a boatload of wonderful benefits and tax advantages, reducing a level of anxiety that should not be there in this relationship or in any other committed relationship.

- One example is the issue of hospital visitation and who is considered "the parent" during crises. Currently, the person who is labeled "mother" or "father" on a child's birth certificate is the one who must deal with the hospital, not necessarily both same-sex parents. There have been plenty of cases in which even when the proper paperwork is produced, hospitals are less than willing to treat partners as parents. This is not the same for heterosexual couples at all.

- Children need to know where parental authority lies. It is clear in our family that the children's biological mom and I have the final word in what goes on in the lives of Parker and Adrianne. This was clarified early on, especially when Dean said he did not want to be known as a step-dad. Of course, this has not stopped him from offering advice. And the children have often turned to Dean as a confidante at times, as a "safe person" to talk to when their parents are struggling to make hard decisions.

- Children and the entire family will feel a sense of equality with straight families. Children experience the second-class citizen status of their gay and lesbian parents because we are not allowed to wed and be in a marriage relationship. With marriage, the children will be grateful for a chance to talk about their two moms or two dads, as well as to complain, gripe, celebrate, laugh, and cry with us. After all, marriage creates "kith and kin" for all of us, gay and straight alike. And it is in these familial bonds that we stick with each other, whether we always like one another or not, because we are, after all, family.

GOOD FOR OUR HEALTH

Studies show that those who are married live healthier lives, physically as well as emotionally, than do single, widowed, or divorced people.[15] This is as true for straight people as it is for gay or lesbian people. Given all the blessings and curses of relationships, being together in holy union may be good for our overall health!

This is in large part because knowing whom we are in relationship which provides stability to our lives. And stability is something we all want to come home to.

The rituals that may strengthen our relationships or stretch them to their very limits are the holidays and the way we celebrate them with family and friends. This is the topic of the next chapter.

7

THE HOLIDAYS ... AND HOW TO SURVIVE THEM

Chekhov wrote (I paraphrase): If you want to understand true loneliness, get married. To which I would add: If you want to understand true childishness, become a parent.

—JESSE GREEN[1]

I enjoy a good party! Why? Because celebrations hold within them the possibility of good cheer, great fun, the exchange of best wishes, a bona fide "bon voyage," and the embodiment of hope and love in tangible, real ways among a group of people who may or may not know one another.

Even the anticipation of a celebration is exciting: the possibility of being surrounded by a bouquet of balloons, bunches of flowers, streamers taped to the ceiling and walls, a banner announcing the event in colorful designs; special tablecloths and utensils; singing or listening to music, perhaps dancing, special food and drinks, and especially a fantastic dessert that is "oohed" and "aahed" by all (preferably chocolate). Celebratory occasions are essential parts of life. I cannot imagine my life without a party or celebratory gathering from time to time. Such milestone affairs mark us, mark our time together, and hold out the possibility of drawing family and friends closer together.

This chapter focuses on how celebrations in a family, household, or community can be both markers and ways to make good memories to savor in the years to come, as well as acknowledging in what ways these festivities can also be a time for drawing us closer together, reinforcing the "ties that bind" us as a family.

THE HOPE OF A PARTY

The hope of a party is that not only will everyone have a good time, but that people will want to come together again, for whatever reason, and celebrate some more. Yet it appears that the heightened expectation of any celebration brings out either the best or the worst in people. There is within us a need to play, to party, no matter our age, gender, or sexual orientation. Celebrations of holidays and other gala occasions that are normally held within and among a family gathering or community hold the potential of being a joyous time of building good and meaningful memories. For gay- and lesbian-headed households, this seems especially true: many of us who are gay or lesbian want to take opportunities to "normalize" our relationships with the rest of society, celebrating the important moments of life as we did before we came out or were aware we were lesbian or gay.

Celebrations also offer us an opportunity to do what *all* families and friends do and need: provide a time of joy, of love, of levity and good cheer with one and all. The need to celebrate, to party, to rejoice, and to build memories from these occasions, to make fools of ourselves for the common and greater good, seems worth it. While some celebrations among gays and straights can sometimes be awkward as we create new rituals, it is also an opportunity to try something new, to reach out and to learn to embrace those among us who seem estranged. Celebrations can create places and times of healing, of renewing and restoring relationships that have been tested from time to time and are now ready to be made stronger and more whole.

THE FEAR OF THE PARTY

On the other hand, we are reminded that these convivial get-togethers can be awkward, if not downright calamitous. The festivities can usher forth a time of difficult emotions and callous, unthinking gestures. Granted, at any social gathering, the social etiquette of our culture is heightened as people try to "be on their best behavior" when there may be little in the way of crisis or conflict. Just imagine what happens when a crisis or conflict is still causing people in the group to be enraged. These very gatherings of heightened expectations and emotions hold within them the possibility of letting the subtle, unspoken biases of a family toward gays and lesbians come bubbling to the surface. It is then that we who are gay or lesbian need to remember that this possible crisis is not necessarily our problem, and may be the problem of the straight people in attendance, who must now face the awkwardness of the social situation.

For example, some of our family members or friends still do not know what to do with "us," gay or lesbian, or with our children, whether we are members of a close extended family or living singly and "unattached." Because of all the stereotypes of lesbians and gays in American society, many of our straight family members and friends simply do not know what to make of us or do with us in a social setting. While perhaps they love us individually as members of a certain family, there are moments of amazing gracelessness: when we are not invited to our partner's family reunion simply because, well, they just don't know what to make of our relationship; or the times that a family gathering goes still and uneasily calm whenever someone wants to talk about the "gay parents" in front of the young children. Strange as it sounds, it is an ongoing problem for many of us who are gay or lesbian.

But the problem is more complex when children are part of the event. It is one thing to treat an adult who is gay or lesbian in such a way. In the presence of our children, the celebrations of birthdays, anniversaries, funerals, memorials, reunions, and special dinners for work are all possible places where social blunders are made, and people wander with little forethought into saying something embarrassing about people who are gay or lesbian, hurting other people without knowing it. Or, worse yet, some people take the opportunity purposely to hurt others in a large social setting.

Finally, there may be a kind of clash of cultures, of communities—gay versus straight—in the middle of life's galas. It may make many of us feel rattled and self-conscious, often causing more than just the host or hostess to feel slightly worried about how the event will be perceived and, later, what memories we will have to either confront or console us when we need to remember the "good days," depending on the turn of events.

To help those who are straight to appreciate what may seem like the peculiar awkwardness of our situation, have them switch places. I would ask the straight person to come to a party or a quiet dinner with others who are gay or lesbian and stay at that party until some of the awkwardness passes. A variation would be to invite the straight person to attend a Gay Pride parade or to come to a Drag Queen bingo event.

The focus of this chapter is the importance of celebrations in the lives of gay- or lesbian-headed households. I will begin with a story of an uncertain Thanksgiving meal that began with some moments of bungling misstatements that later became moments of quiet and genuine goodness.

CELEBRATIONS!

Celebration of holidays, birthdays, and anniversaries are important in a person's, a couple's, and a family's life. We learn much about ourselves, especially about our preferences and biases, likes and dislikes, through the celebrations we share.

For example, we learn what kind of food everyone prefers by the platters and snack trays that are brought. During discussions over a meal, we learn about the activities that occupy the time of the other diners. For those who feel or believe there is a need for a prayer before a meal, we learn about the beliefs of that family or community. What people wear to such a gathering, the topics of conversation, all help to reveal who they are. Even the people we invite to our celebrations says something about us, revealing those whose company we enjoy. Or the invitation list could reflect the host or hostess's attempt to bring together interesting people who warm hearts, stretch minds and imaginations. Inviting a stranger into our midst for a meal is always an opportunity to imagine the world differently.

All celebrations of holidays, birthdays, anniversaries, and the like have three movements:

- Parties and celebrations remind us of things past. Parties and celebrations always have the potential to remind us of people in the past, and wonderful or awkward memories of days gone by. Just a song sung, a tune played, a word spoken, a smell or aroma blows embers upon our memories and brings back feelings that we may have thought were once gone or hidden. Bringing out a photo album, replaying an old eight-millimeter film, showing an old video, or playing a record album from a bygone era can all evoke memories that, for a moment, inter-ject themselves into today.

We first learn about parties and celebrations when we are growing up. In turn, we add our own variation upon the theme of what is a "party" or "celebration." The food that we offer, the songs that we sing, the games that we play, the places where we gather for a meal, are decisions and choices based on the experiences of our early years. In other words, our ability to celebrate has been taught to us and is indicative of a long-ago place, time, and people.

The importance of teaching our childen to celebrate cannot be underestimated. I have been with people who have been shaped by families or groups who could or would not celebrate. Many of us have relationships with people who were not raised in homes or families or kinship networks and who simply did not celebrate much if anything of life, thus leaving them bereft.

The obverse is true as well: we keep on learning anew the importance of celebrating some of the "highlights" of life by remembering to celebrate such moments when they come along. There is something important about just letting your-self go and having a fabulous time doing it.

- Celebrations have a way of focusing or intensifying things. I have come to appreciate that we learn how to celebrate a birth-day, an anniversary, or a holiday from those with whom we live. Every time we have a celebration of any kind in our household, we remind one another of the gift of play and the importance of playing together, which can either unite people or divide them. Whether we are hurling rice or bird seed at a wedding or at a same-sex union, blowing up balloons, creating a punch that no one has tasted before, playing Marco Polo, splashing water at a pool party or in the ocean somewhere, singing songs or dancing to the rhythm of disco at a 1970s party, in such play, in such celebrations, we are teaching one another the art of partying and living life to its fullest *in the present moment.*

Sometimes we need such signifiers, such symbols, such created milestones to be sure to remember the life we live today. We share the birthday of someone living with HIV/AIDS, knowing that there will be a day when he or she will no longer be present in our midst, but will remain alive in our memories. We gather at a meal with friends who are about to move away, knowing this will be the last time we will enjoy a regular occasional meal together. We call friends and family members on their birthdays or anniversaries, just to let them know they are remembered. The celebrations of today build memories for the future.

- Celebrations held today become memories of tomorrow as soon as they happen in the "today-ness" of life. It is thoroughly unexpected but wonderful when the celebrations of one day become memories the very next day. I have been in many family gatherings the day after such a celebration as we remember where we were, who we were with, and exactly what was said by whom just a day earlier. Celebrations and parties then slowly to fade into the inner recesses of our collective and individual beings.

THE WAY WE WERE, THE WAY WE ARE, AND THE WAY WE COULD BE: STRATEGIES FOR ENJOYING CELEBRATIONS!

For gay parents, celebrations and parties are also important for building new ways to celebrate our family relationships. As stated above, in celebrations, we learn a lot about who we are, our likes, dislikes, preferences, biases, and also on.

In order to make celebrations a happy event for all involved, consider the following strategies. First, if you are "new" to being an "out" gay or lesbian family, then find another "out" gay or lesbian family and be part of their holiday celebration. Learn all their customs, rituals, and ways of celebrating life. If we mark time and important benchmarks in life with celebrations, it's important to find out how other lesbian and gay couples do it with their families.

Second, go small and build up. I have found that some of the celebrations and rituals of life that are done on grand scales in some homes and families can easily be reduced to smaller affairs. For example, while I have been to some grand Christmas feasts with my family, I have learned that what we all liked the most was a tradition born in England, in which we pass around "crackers," round tubes with colorful paper wrapped around them, that, when pulled, "snap" or "crack," and, when opened, provide us with paper hats, games, puzzles, and slips of papers containing jokes. We have many photos of family members wearing such hats around the dinner table in both my house and at the home of my former wife. What is most important is making the effort to mark occasions that shape and name us as a family.

Third, carrying on with generalized traditional celebrations from our faith communities can also be quite helpful in enabling us to feel "plugged in" with others during celebrations and holidays. In the best of all worlds, church holidays, high holy days, are hopefully practiced at home as well as at church. For example, using Advent and Lenten devotionals at home as well as at church can tie us into the broader life of the Church.

Fourth, simply remembering the occasion of someone's life is enough for a celebration: a homemade card, a small cupcake, and a candle may be all that is needed. It is remembering whose and who we are.

Finally, our celebrations should include not just our immediate families or other gay and lesbian families, but should be shared with families in which straight couples may also be the parents. In other words, integration is good for all. Celebrations can be times for us to make new friends and normalize relationships with other families and neighbors—who must wonder from time to time, "So, what *does* a gay- or lesbian-headed household look like?"

This building of friendship networks is the theme of the next chapter.

8

FRIENDS ... AND THEIR PARENTS

Friendship is one of the greatest gifts a human
being can receive.
Friendship makes all of life shine brightly.
Blessed are those who lay down their lives for
their friends.

—HENRI NOUWEN[1]

Much of what we learned in life happened somewhere around kindergarten ... or that's what Robert Fulghum had many of us thinking in the 1980s with his book *All I Really Need to Know I Learned in Kindergarten.*[2] In kindergarten and in the early primary grades, especially during periods like recess and show-and-tell, we share stories, and, during lunch and snack time, we learn the ins and outs of friendship and relationships, both with children our age, and with people in authority, like parents and teachers. We also learn how to play fair, to follow the rules, and to step into school and schoolyard rituals and stories. And we learn what it means to live and work toward the common good. Quite a lot happens in a young child's life.

On playgrounds and sport fields, during times of fellowship and celebrations, rituals and social gatherings, worship and service projects in church, we develop skills that allow us to relate to and be friends with one another. As we participate in the give-and-take of games ... and the games of life, we discover the attitudes, perceptions, biases, prejudices, and ideals of our friends and acquaintances. We also learn virtues like self-control, patience, and charity, to name a few, that are also taught in communities of faith. The attitudes and the virtues we first learn on the playground extend into our families as gay and lesbian couples and parents.

For example, when I worked as an advocate with and for people with disabilities, I would teach the "naming" and the history of names of people with disabilities and look at how the names reflect the general attitude toward, concept of, or perception of people with disabilities. Usually in school or on athletic fields, during recess or during lunch, we learned and taught one another names for people with disabilities, such as: crip, spaz, tard, retard, idiot, feeble-minded, simp, and gimp, to name a few. Seeing the reactions to my putting these names up on the wall was like watching a cartoon lightbulb go on in people's minds. They immediately understood that the prejudice and bias we have against people with disabilities start at an early age and that no one puts a stop to the name-calling. Although playgrounds and friendships build up community, they also plant the seeds of its destruction.

Likewise, during play—during a school recess period, at a playground, or on an athletic field—is when derogatory words come out for gays and lesbians as well. And like other minority groups in America, we've taken those names and, in our own way, made them our own. Early on in life I heard some of the derogatory comments, and, as my children have told me, these very same comments are mouthed on today's playgrounds (and in other venues) too: faggot, gay (as in "That's so gay"), queer, queer-bait, poofter, butch, fairy, dyke, lesbo, lesbionic, a twinkie, princess; pussy, wimp, bent wrist; chicken hawk, and wus, to name a few. Here again, we learn these derogatory names at a young age and avoid anything that could "tar and feather us" with them. The seeds of homophobia are well planted as we do what we can later in life not to be named as "a homosexual," "queer," or "gay."

Name-calling among youth, along with encouraging bullying, damages the very fabric of our communities, careers, neighborhoods, the country, its churches and social groups. The attitudes and associated practices of prejudice against gays and lesbians are later cemented in the limited imaginations of many people who dare not step outside the bounds of what is deemed "normal" and "appropriate behavior." More to the point, my children hear these very same derogatory terms and then come home, turn around, and see that their dad is "one of those."

As a defense mechanism of sorts, some in the LGBT community have terms for straight people, like "breeders," but they do not seem as problematic or dangerous and usually are ignored. Oftentimes, we can turn one of these phrases on its head, because the context in which some phrases are heard, for example, "That's so gay!" does matter. One night, while Dean and I were preparing dinner, Parker unexpectedly said, "What I like about coming to this house is I can say 'That's so gay,' and you are both okay with it, and like it. How cool is that!"

We who are LGTB want to make sure that we are afforded all the rights and privileges of living in this society in general, as well as in the church in particular, that people who are straight enjoy and sometimes seem to take for granted. Under the U.S. Constitution and the Bill of Rights, we know that we have the right to marry; to not be discriminated against in housing and employment simply because we are American citizens; and to pursue life, liberty, and happiness, like all other citizens. Likewise, we seek to be full members of the body of Christ in our respective churches, and believe that if God calls us to ministry and service, we should be not be discriminated against in pursuing this call simply because we are LGBT. And, like all citizens, and all members of churches, we know that we must be law-abiding, contributing members of society, and faithful in our discipleship in a church.

The place where this kind of movement toward being fully embraced by society and a church community is not necessarily by the power of state or federal laws alone per se, though some laws can change people's behaviors for the good. What is even more powerful in changing people's behaviors and heart are relationships and friendships that have with one another. The change that matters most is change of heart, of attitude of self and community. And this kind of change comes through relationships, through friendships. Because it is in the "school of friendship" that we learn the virtues that undergird and lead us toward understanding others and working toward the common good of all.

RELATIONSHIPS CHANGE LIVES, POLITICS, AND THEOLOGY

The politics of the state, as well as the politics of a church, can be shaped through and in the friendships and acquaintances that we have in life.

For example, in politics, I was impressed by the story of State Senator Gale Candaras, a Democrat from Wilbraham, Massachusetts. Earlier in 2007, Senator Candaras was ready to vote for a constitutional ban against gays and lesbians being allowed to be married. But what changed her mind, and her vote, in which she chose not to vote for the constitutional ban, were relationships:

> I know from listening to my constituents, since I first became Senator this year that this vote, the vote I take today, is the right vote for the people I serve. I have been most impressed by

the number of individuals who have called me and asked me to change my vote because they have changed their minds. One grandmother told me she had changed her mind and wanted me to change my vote in case one of her grandchildren grew up to be gay or lesbian. She did not want any of her grandchildren to be denied the right to marry the person they love. This is exactly the legacy we will leave to generations beyond us, and the example we can set for the nation and, I daresay the world, which is certainly paying attention to what we do and say here today.

I also want to address directly one of the more contentious issues in this debate: Same gender couples have been adopting children and building families here in the Commonwealth for about twenty years. In many instances, same gendered couples have adopted children with severe challenges, children no one else wanted, and they have worked miracles with them. These children would have lived lives of despair without these families. This underscores how we cannot afford to marginalize any of our people; make anyone second-class citizens. We are all precious resources to each other, and to generations yet to come.[3]

Senator Candaras changed her vote because of the people who took the time to call and relate their stories to her ... and they became her friends.

Likewise in the church, those churches—pastors, priests, lay leaders, religious leaders, and laity—who have opened their hearts, minds, and congregations to people who are LGBT often do so because of relationships with gays or lesbians.

FRIENDSHIPS CLOSE TO HOME

One aspect of family life that Dean and I keep working on concerns our friendships as family members. To be more precise, the friendships that matter are the friends we have as a couple; friendships that the children have with other children; and friendships we have with other families.

Because I was outed involuntarily as a gay person and was denied tenure at Duke University, there was a precipitous drop in my social life, which also affected the children. For example, *before* I was outed, we were welcome to all faculty-sponsored family events at Duke Divinity School. *After* I was outed, my children and I were no longer invited to any family events held by other faculty members. Friends who knew the professor who outed me stopped all contact immediately. Lines had been drawn; connections had been severed as if it had all happened in the dark of night. At national conferences, people I did not know well but were acquaintances with would either duck and avoid me or simply smile empathetically and say, "I'm so sorry. I heard about what happened"—without asking me about what happened. While new friends and acquaintances have since emerged, and while some truly good friends showed their mettle by remaining my friends, those who were part of "that world" wrote no good-bye notes or e-mails, but simply stopped communicating with me.

My friendship circle was not the only one that changed; so did my children's. People in their public schools, in church, and in other social groups knew I was gay and leaving my wife "for a man!" I found out that once my story was told by one other person, it was no longer private or a secret and it was no longer my story. It was out in the world to be shared with others. And share it they did! Chapel Hill, Carrboro, Durham, and Raleigh are still small Southern towns, no matter how many émigrés come into these places from the North (in other words, Yankees) or other places in the world. A professor being denied tenure by Duke Divinity School and questions around it concerning his being gay was serious gossip fodder.

While I became accustomed to being ignored by certain former friends, my children were also treated differently. But their friends didn't treat them differently, the *parents* of their friends treated them differently, and ostracized them. For example, among my daughter's friends we had this common phenomenon: Adrianne would invite a friend to come and sleep over at our house. The parent would say no to the request for the child to sleep over at our house, but would say yes to sleeping at my former wife's house. This pattern continued even with birthday parties. A parent would find out that my daughter's birthday party was at our house—where the homos lived—and the child would not be able to come. But if the party was held at my former wife's house, the same child had the parent's permission to come.

FRIENDSHIPS IN CONGREGATIONS

Again, as I would tell congregants in talks about people with disabilities, we all know someone in our lives who is disabled. And it's the same with us. Everyone in a congregation or parish knows someone who is a lesbian, gay, bisexual, or transgendered person, whether the LBGT person admits it or the church member realizes it. Homophobia is a powerful, stealthy, and foggy presence, cloaking and hiding us not only from ourselves, but from each other.

Many church-related groups of LGBT people have moved toward establishing friendships and relationships with congregants and parishioners—some of whom are friendly or some not so friendly. In discussions with several leaders of Metropolitan Community Church, Soulforce, and LGBT church-related groups such as More Light Presbyterians (Presbyterian Church [USA]), Reconciling Ministries (United Methodists), Dignity (Roman Catholics), and Integrity (Episcopalians), I found that they have perfected building relationships wherever possible in individual churches within their own denominations as well as establishing networks with similar groups from other denominations. For example, at conferences and retreats on subjects that may be tangentially related to LGBT issues, there will be an information table with brochures about LGBT people in the church. General annual meetings always have an open-invitation dinner and rallies along with reports, bills, and amendments being discussed and voted on; the more general events are logical places for LGBT people to make church contacts. I have watched teams of LGBT people go into churches where they would not necessarily be welcomed and try to make connections. I have seen leaders in my own denomination thinking strategically and wanting to enter into worthwhile conversations, like the Rev. Dr. Jack Rogers, former moderator of the Presbyterian Church (USA), who has met with and engaged in Bible study with those opposed to the ordination of lesbians and gay. Money to continue the discussion is also important, because such work is itself a full-time occupation; printing brochures, sending mass mailings, and having an Internet presence are all part of building and sustaining the movement.

After all is said and done, acceptance of LGBT people by churches still boils down to the relationships that we have with one another in which we learn the virtues necessary to change for the common good of *all* people, regardless of sexual orientation. In the next section, the focus is on friendships and on the kinds of friends we need as active participants in our lives.

FRIENDSHIPS

It will be through friendships and acquaintances that we change the public's and churches' perception of gay and lesbian families. And the beauty of friendship, according to philosophers like Aristotle and theologians like St. Thomas Aquinas, is that it is a relationship based upon mutual self-giving, making each person a better person simply because of their friendship with each another. Indeed, the success or the failure of one person in the relationship could account for the success or failure of the other person in the relationship.[4] Not only is friendship a school for learning the virtues, thus shaping our very character, but friendship may be considered to be a virtue unto itself, as we practice and come to know what is "good" in another and become a good or better person through our relationship with him or her.

To understand better the importance of our friendships, whether as a couple, with our children, and with our entire family in relationship with other families like ours and with those not like ours, let us consider the meaning of friendships, using Aristotle's three kinds of friendship.

- *Acquaintances:* These are people with whom we have relationships of utility. For example, the person who works on the car, the travel agent who sells us airplane tickets, the checkout clerk at the supermarket with whom we exchange pleasantries—these are people who help us. We also complain to them the phone when we are overbilled and quarrel with them when they don't give us the correct change after a cash purchase. This kind of friendship may include coworkers, employees, and employers as well.

- *Mutual friends:* As we make our way to the bar or to the movies or gather together in our church book group or stamp club, we are surrounded by mutual buddies. Time spent with these people, telling stories, discussing a book, talking about events of the day at the edge of the YMCA pool, is meaningful and fruitful, but we spend little time thinking about each other when we are apart. We can have many of these relationships, for they come and go quite easily.

- *True companions:* This friendship is a deeply satisfying relationship in which each person cares about the good of the other. The kind of relationship endures because the motive behind it is the care of the other, of the friend. This might be called true friendship. These friendships are rare because they involve the entirety of one's being in meaningful relationship.

It has been my experience that the last kind of friendship, while ideal for the gay or lesbian couple in a relationship, is always a work in progress, always needing to be tended to, such as a garden or anything organic in nature. There are many gay and lesbian couples who have the second kind of friendship, who have come together as friends who enjoy each other's company but, when they are no longer in each other's company, the connection is not necessarily there.

Likewise with our children. Some gay and lesbian couples are friends with their children in the most meaningful way, while other gay and lesbian parents do not necessarily have the time or are willing to find the time to create and maintain a deep, abiding relationship.

As for acquaintances, they are to be found at conferences, for example, whether while walking on the beach in Provincetown, Massachusetts, during the first weekend in August for the COLAGE gathering, at the National Gay Lesbian Task Force "Creating Change" annual gathering, or at a church assembly or a diocesan meeting.

Why this focus on friendship? Not only will our relationships and friendships change the way we know one another, but all three kinds of relationships in our life keep us going when the going gets tough. First, when I have felt emotionally spent after being assaulted by a church member because I am gay; when I read yet another pronouncement from a church body telling me what a "family" is, and it isn't my family; when I turn on the news to watch LGBT people treated as an "interesting minority group" among the many others, worthy of airing a special on "us" while "they" draw their own psychological conclusions—I am ready for all the kinds of friendship that energize me, and us, and enable us to live one more day.

Secondly, there is truth to the axiom "strength in numbers." When I attend Pride events in North Carolina, visit booths of LGBT material in a church assembly, see a rainbow sticker on someone else's car other than my own in the rural part of North Carolina, I have a sense of "I/we are not alone in this world."

In the next section, I want to focus on how our friendships can help make our churches in particular, and the world in general, a more hospitable place not only for us, but for *all* families. After all, hospitality is a virtue learned within the context of friendship.

STRATEGIES

- *Coming out to friends:* In chapter two, I discussed strategies and circles of people in our immediate families to whom we need to "come out," telling them, "I am gay" or "I am lesbian." The other group that we need to come out to is our friends, close friends as well as mere acquaintances. As I wrote above, I was surprised at the number of my former friends who simply stopped communicating with me when I was outed involuntarily, but I have made other friends since then, as have Dean and my children.

  Coming out to close friends is as important, sometimes more important, than coming out to family members. Sometimes, by first telling friends that we are gay or lesbian, we can come out more easily to our family members. Call it a trial run. In my case, one of the first questions friends ask is, "Do the children know you're gay?" Yes.

- *Making friends:* While some people who are gay or lesbian talk about the host of new friends they make once they come out of the "closet," many others talk about the loneliness that still haunts us at times, no matter what our age when we came out.

  A shocking number of gay and lesbian youth have contemplated or committed suicide around issues of being gay or lesbian in this heterosexual world. Likewise, probably many women and men have not "come out" and have stayed in marriages or have remained in their "closet" for fear of coming out and how they would be received by family and friends.

The act and art of making friends is natural for some and awkward for others. It is important that we teach one another the art of making connections with others, especially when they are feeling fragile and alone in the coming-out process. Our children, let alone our partners, may not always appreciate the changes that occur when we come out in public; they may not understand being gay or lesbian in a culture that is not caring or sensitive to the issues we face daily. Sympathetic friends can help.

MAINTAINING FRIENDSHIPS: HANGING OUT WITH PEOPLE JUST LIKE US

As mentioned above, there is such a thing as "strength in numbers." There is something strangely wonderful about walking into a ballroom in a hotel for a conference with people like me, a dad who is Christian, gay with kids, and in a partnered relationship, all still living at home. It is wonderful to share stories, to see what is going on in other people's lives, to connect the dots of the sane and insane moments of being a gay dad in a partnered relationship. These are moments of "drinking from a well that gives life," which we must do from time to time.

BROADENING THE CIRCLE OF FRIENDSHIPS BEYOND OUR COMFORT ZONE

Likewise, it is helpful to come out of our comfort zones and hang out with people who are not like us, with straight people, and talk with them about our lives and listen as they talk about theirs. Chances are, we both hold stereotypes about each other, and it is important to get beyond the labels and stereotypes and to get to know people.

For example, two lesbian moms I know who had their son in a preschool program in Chapel Hill talked about taking their child not to a preschool run by a lesbian couple down the street, but to a church preschool. Why? They wanted the child to be exposed not only to families like theirs, but also to families who are from Africa and Korea, as well as to be with children with disabilities.

With a conscious effort to push ourselves beyond the comfort zone, we start to build bridges and connections in relationships to change the world. Making these connections with strangers who could become good friends could possibly change the world in which we live. If not, at least you may make a new friend.

IN THE END, STRIVING FOR THE COMMON GOOD OF ALL

In the masterful study *Habits of the Heart*,[5] the authors looked at individualism and the phenomenon of community, which is currently what holds us together as a people in this country as well as in our churches. Through the "habits of the heart" that we are taught in our relationships and friendships, we may be able to make significant changes in our families, our communities, our states, and our nation. But change will happen not by grand strategies from "on high," but through the grassroots efforts of people who grab a cup of coffee not for one but for two, who sit down across from a stranger and begin to talk about the mundane aspects of life, slowly uncovering commonalities. They discover that what we share in common is greater than our differences, straight versus gay, that some would like to use in keeping us apart.

9

~~

LEGAL POTPOURRI

The quest for gay marriage, then, is not only about civil rights for gays and lesbians, but also about legal and social recognition for their families.

—WILLIAM STACY JOHNSON[1]

SEPARATION AND DIVORCE

The first time I ever needed a lawyer was when I was in the process of separating and divorcing from my former wife. Up to that time, I had only needed to talk with an attorney when I was buying or selling a house. But then I did not need to worry about the law and its effect upon my life.

Upon receiving the separation papers, taken aback but moving forward in life, I hired a family-divorce attorney, who looked over the documents with me. Although the paperwork was fairly formulaic, I knew that in the State of North Carolina I had very little in the way of support for my side as a dad because I am gay.

Pam, as the heterosexual woman and the mother of our children, had not only the law but probably any judge and jury in the state on her side of the discussion. There are no laws in the State of North Carolina that are necessarily supportive of gay or lesbian parents. Instead, there have been cases in North Carolina in which married men who are gay and in relationships with other men during a marriage lost not only their marriage but their children, because the law especially frowns upon LGBT people in such cases.[2]

With some relief to both of us, Pam and I talked together— outside of an attorney's office—and we came to an agreement about our separation: joint legal custody and joint physical custody. How did this happen? We both deeply want our children to grow up in an environment in which love prevails, and not in one of antagonism and malice. Some days we accomplish this better than other days.

Sadly, this would not be the only time I would turn to a lawyer or a legal firm. Our separation agreement was merely an introduction. The next crisis in my life was a protracted battle over the nondiscrimination policy of my then employer. In three years' time, I had two different attorneys and consulted with law firms in three different parts of North Carolina, along with consulting people at Human Rights Campaign and Lambda Legal Services. To make a long story short, what I learned was that while private companies—and a university is considered a private company— can *write* a nondiscrimination policy that includes protections based on sexual orientation, since there is no force of state and/or federal law, the private employers can follow the nondiscrimination policy when they want to and can decide to withhold it or not implement it.

What did this lack of legal protection in terms of discrimination have upon my life? I lost the income that I was earning, which was good for university pay. I lost how much my retirement package could have accumulated. I lost the benefit of financial remuneration for my children's college tuition (a benefit that many lesbians and gays argued against because many of them do not have children). My partner and I lost some of the medical and dental coverage we had. I lost the rights to use health facilities on campus. In other words, I lost all the rights and privileges I had as a university employee because there was no employee protection, because there are no state or federal laws, such as the Employment Non-Discrimination Act (ENDA), to force the university's hand.

POTPOURRI OF LEGAL ISSUES

Even though I am trained as a Presbyterian pastor, knowing the many competitive interpretations from our *Book of Order*, I was not as savvy as I have become in understanding the law and in reading between the lines of legal opinions and judgments. Because the laws of North Carolina are never on the side of gay fathers or lesbian moms when it comes to child custody, I was reluctant to proceed with coming out of the closet, which meant leaving my physical home (but not my responsibilities as a father to my children) to live truthfully and honestly in a relationship with another man. As the state controls and regulates our personal relationships, our families are shaped in large part by legal parameters and precedents.[3]

I call this chapter "Legal Potpourri," a collection of miscellaneous legal issues, because the many laws that affect those of us who are gay and lesbian are wide-ranging and yet specific to our various stories, depending on where we work, where we live, what state we reside in, and what federal laws protect us ... or don't, as the case may be. Many other books go into greater depth and detail and include the history of laws pertaining to marriage and adoption, as well as issues surrounding mixed racial marriages ("miscegenation"), for example, which was illegal in American society up to the 1950s.

The list of legal issues that follows is not exhaustive. These are merely issues that my friends and acquaintances and I keep running up against that have thwarted our ability to live lives with a sense of peace and calm when it comes to the laws of the land. While there have been some milestone legal events in recent times such as *Lawrence vs. Texas*, in reality, there is little in the way of civil legal protection to cover and protect us as LGBT people living in the United States.

MARRIAGE AND SAME-SEX CIVIL UNIONS

In 1992, in the state of Colorado, Amendment 2, which restricted civil rights of LGBT people, passed, but it was overturned in 1996. However, in 1996, then-President Clinton signed into law the Defense of Marriage Act, DOMA, which stated that marriage shall be between one man and one woman. This was largely in response to the 1993 legal case *Baehr vs. Miike of Hawaii*, in which the plaintiffs were hoping that Hawaii would be the first state to allow same-sex marriage. Hawaii had decided that denying same-sex couples a marriage license violated the state constitution.[4]

However, in 2000, in the State of Vermont, same-sex unions were allowed and made legal with a law signed by then-Governor Howard Dean. Same-sex partners in that state have all the rights and privileges as opposite-sex partners have, but these are not generalized into federal rights and responsibilities of marriage, especially in terms of Social Security and taxes, to say the least.

In 2004, the State of Massachusetts became the first state in the Union, by an act of the state supreme court, to say that gay and lesbian couples could get married. However, couples married in Massachusetts could go home and be unmarried in places like North Carolina.

In 2005, Connecticut became another state that allowed same-sex couples an opportunity to have relationships recognized legally; in 2006, Reformed Judaism allowed rabbis to hold same-sex union services; and in 2007, New Hampshire and New Jersey joined the other states in providing civil protections for same-sex couples, while Washington state now permits same-sex adoption, and is moving quickly to allow same-sex unions as well.

POWER OF ATTORNEY: LAST WILL AND TESTAMENT

Because we do not have the same protections under the law as straight couples, missing out on the 1,138 federal ways that we could be protected like straight couples are by the laws of the United States,[5] we have to pay for legal services in order to protect ourselves, including the creation of wills and to ensure that what we own in common remains so in the event that one partner is hurt, incapacitated, or dies.

On a recent trip to the Middle East, my partner and I (finally) wrote our wills. While heterosexual couples should be sure to do this as well, it is imperative, especially when children are involved, for gay couples to register their wills with the local county authorities. Without a will, if I were to die my possessions would be treated as if I were single, my children would be taxed on the inheritance, and my partner—with whom I hold much in common legally, such as our house, funds, and cars—would not necessarily have the protection necessary for procuring or retaining them. Heterosexual couples are more likely to have financial security if one of them dies, but the same cannot be said for gay or lesbian couples. The right to inheritance and to other resources has to be spelled out, in a legally binding document, for gay and lesbian couples to protect themselves and their children.

MEDICAL COVERAGE

Medical coverage differs for couples and families depending on the employer. For example, my partner *did* receive same-sex partner benefits for health and dental coverage while I worked at Duke, but I am not covered by his employer's medical and dental benefits. Meanwhile, in our divorce agreement, my former wife and I decided that the children would be under my health and dental coverage.

However, where we also need coverage, both for ourselves and for our children, has to do with basic rights of hospital visitation. It is important that lesbian and gay couples obtain the necessary legal powers to visit, as a family member would, when one of partners is ill and in the hospital. These papers need to be always at hand, because many hospitals demand proof that we are a couple—unlike heterosexual couples, who do not have to show such papers, only a wedding ring and perhaps a driver's license. Many couples have had to have legal papers faxed proving that one partner can make the medical decisions for the other partner when hospitalized faraway.

Second, paperwork needs to be available at all times stating that either partner can make decisions regarding a child's treatment in a doctor's or dentist's office or in the case of hospitalization. In our case, my partner needs my permission to make decisions regarding my children when he takes them to the doctor or the dentist. Likewise, for some gay or lesbian couples, the person who is not the one who adopted the child or mothered the child needs proof of identification and/or papers legitimating his or her power to make decisions.

ADOPTION, FOSTER PROGRAMS, AND FERTILIZATION

Along with my "head of household" designation, the other tax advantage that I have as the father of someone who is under the age of eighteen is the child tax credit. In creating families, many lesbian and gay couples turn to various forms of bringing a child into their families: adoption, foster children, and, with the help of modern medicine, birth. This is how more of us are now heads of household and are able to profit from the child tax credit—small consolation since we cannot get any of the other benefits of being married under the programs of the federal government.

Many couples are turning to adoption, choosing at times to adopt older children, some with behavioral, developmental, emotional, or physical disabilities, in the States. Other couples are applying for adoption in China, Vietnam, Guatemala, Russia, Romania, and other countries around the world. In some countries, a gay or lesbian couple is not allowed to adopt; only one member of the couple can adopt because the laws of the country of the adoptee. Of course, like any straight couple, the lesbian and gay couple will also have to deal with the culture clash that may come in later years if the adopted child is of a different race, ethnicity, or heritage than the parents.

Some adoption possibilities but also obstacles abound in the States. According to Taylor Gandossy:

> Three states have laws denying gays and lesbians the right to adopt or take in foster children. Though Mississippi allows single gays and lesbians to adopt, it prohibits same-sex couples from adopting. Utah excludes same-sex couples indirectly through a statute barring all unmarried couples from adopting or taking in foster children. Florida is currently the only state that specifically bans "homosexual" individuals from adopting, although the state does allow them to be foster parents.[6]

However, other states allow judges, adoption services, and foster agencies to make decisions regarding gay and lesbian couples adopting or becoming foster parents. For example, in the case of Dan Savage and his partner,[7] they knew the birth mother of their child, having (kind of) both chosen each other through a service for mothers and couples who are looking to adopt. These open adoptions are becoming more popular among gay and lesbian couples. While some couples choose to adopt a child outright, others adopt a child after serving as foster parents for some time. This also offers a couple an opportunity to get to know their foster child's family before they adopt him or her. I find it almost heroic that so many gay and lesbian couples have chosen to be foster parents or to adopt children with physical or mental disabilities or other limitations—in other words, children that straight parents might not necessarily choose. In recent years, however, child adoption services run by religious organizations such as the Catholic Church have made it nigh to impossible for LGBT couples to adopt because the church sees such couples as immoral.

Many lesbian couples have chosen to use some form of insemination to become parents.[8] Using sperm banks, many lesbian couples have had in-vitro fertilization. In fact, lesbian couples first raised the issues covered in much of this book since they were the ones using medical methods to become pregnant. As some books have pointed out, there is also an issue between lesbian partners regarding who is the biological mother of the child or children; the other parent is seen as "adopting" the child of the birth mother. Other lesbian couples decide that each partner will have a child, and they share the responsibilities of raising the children together.[9]

Many lesbian women and lesbian couples choose not to use a sperm bank—often because of health concerns (for example, not knowing if the sperm is completely cleared of HIV virus)—but instead, invite a male friend to be a donor! Some lesbian couples simply ask a male friend, or even a gay couple, to consider being the sperm donor, often offering the man or the couple the rights and privileges of co-parenting the child.

Once children have been born into families of gays and lesbians, there is a great need for gay and lesbian couples to get together with other such couples to talk about the ins and outs, ups and downs of raising children in gay- and lesbian-headed families in largely heterosexual America. Meanwhile, through programs like COLAGE, children can be in touch with other children whose parents are gay or lesbian.

Along with these activities, there are more opportunities to let other families know we exist. Through networking with other families over the Internet and taking opportunities to visit with one another, we can take ourselves out of our large closets and no longer be closeted families. In discussions with neighbors, at family gatherings, at work, board meetings, church councils, and school meetings, while other straight parents are talking about their families, we need to talk about our families. We need to be part of our communities rather than being homophobic, denying that we even exist. It isn't until we lesbian and gay parents do this, in front of our children who will witness our bravery, that we will begin to be accepted parts of the communities in which we live, work, and have our being. In a way, the challenge is to "normalize": to make being part of a gay- or lesbian-headed household as normal as apple pie, moms and dads, and whatever sport team you like (along with a dance company, a Broadway show, or a hardware store).

LEGAL SEPARATION AND DIVORCE

There are few laws in the various states that help a gay or lesbian couple work through the issues of separation and divorce, though this number is rising depending on the state where someone resides. Some people follow contract law to figure out how to separate not only property, but also child visitation.

Because many of us have drawn up documents that cover us in case we face an emergency in life, like any other legal document, our separation (it cannot be a divorce unless we are married, and thus are living in Massachusetts) should be handled like any other separation and divorce.

EMPLOYMENT DISCRIMINATION BASED ON SEXUAL ORIENTATION

As stated above, until there are state and federal laws protecting LGBT people from discrimination for being who we are, none of us in the American work force should feel totally safe. While we may believe that we work for a company that does not discriminate against us because we are lesbian, gay, bisexual, or transgendered because there is a written, company-wide policy against such discrimination, it should be known that this policy is executable at will by those who run the company. Because there is no state or federal law pushing employers to support a nondiscrimination policy, a company can, at any time, decide to discriminate based on sexual orientation; thus, the LGBT person can be fired for simply being LGBT.

It is not comforting for those of us who are LGBT to know that we can still be fired or let go for simply being who we are. Our stock portfolios, our retirement benefits, our health care plans—that affect us, our partners, and our children—can all be taken. Many LGBT people play it safe at work, not wanting to make much ado about being LGBT for fear that if they do make a lot of noise or fuss about *anything* in their job, they could be fired simply for being LGBT. Until there are state and federal laws protecting our employment as gay, lesbian, bisexual, and transgendered people, there is nothing to stop a company from firing us for being who we are.

IMMIGRATION LAW AND AIDS

The last law I will discuss here has to do with marriage and partnership in regards to procuring citizenship for an LGBT person from abroad. For heterosexual couples, if one party is from another country, he or she can apply for citizenship based on being married to an American citizen. LGBT people are not offered the same option. If your partner comes from abroad, he or she must often procure extensive visas to stay in this country. Citizenship is not "automatic" simply because you are in a long-term relationship. Citizenship is not automatic for a man or a woman just because he or she is married to an American citizen; however, the process is less onerous and the waiting period is shorter. Likewise, the children of gay and lesbian couples are not automatically citizens of this country unless they are born here.

And if your partner is living with HIV, then citizenship is nearly impossible. Such are the draconian laws of the land.

BEING CREATIVE

As gay and lesbian couples, we are on a unique pilgrimage, marked by legal and civic strides, some setbacks, but with forward motion nonetheless. Without laws in place, we are creating legal protections through individual acts and pioneering the way forward for other minority groups. And while many states have recently voted into law certain constitutional amendments that prohibit us from being legally married, these very laws and amendments can be overturned once cooler heads and kinder hearts prevail. Just remember Prohibition!

10

⌒∾

ON MAKING A
FUTURE TOGETHER

On or around Father's Day several years ago, I broke down and bought one of Brian Andreas's colorful watercolor reproductions. It isn't Brian's art that always draws my attention: I am drawn to the witty, pithy statements that give rise to the art. The statement on the print captured what it has felt like for me to be a dad, especially a gay dad: "I used to believe my father about everything. But then I had children myself and now I see how much stuff you make up just to keep yourself from going crazy."[1]

Being a father or a parent is, in and of itself, a full-time "calling" in the biblical sense of the word. Frederick Buechner has given us the best definition for the term, "calling" or "vocation": "the place God calls you to is the place where your deep gladness and the world's deep hunger meet."[2] Not everyone is called to fatherhood, which is true even among married heterosexual couples. Our script for being fathers is written not only by our very own fathers, but by all the men who have either portrayed fathers in the media, or friends who are fathers or men in stories we have read about fathers. For Christians, God is the paradigmatic parent, the Father, as Jesus calls God, who is a model for being a father, as are stories of fatherhood, like the parable of the Prodigal Son (Luke 15). What we are looking for when a child comes into our lives is what Anne Lamott once called the operating instructions, the manual that should come with every child born on this planet.[3]

Unfortunately—or fortunately, for those who are more creative—there is no such rulebook for being a dad. And the rulebook for gay dads is always in the midst of being created. That is why we struggle, as dads and as parents in general, with all the rules, functions, and expectations of parenthood that change daily, if not hour-by-hour, and sometimes shorter, depending on the circumstances in which child and parent find themselves. We who are dads and moms are called to do so much throughout the days and weeks for, with, and in spite of our child or children, no matter what the child's age. While some of the apron strings—which are attached to moms and dads alike in this egalitarian age—are not as tight as they were when the child—and we—were younger, nonetheless, there is always a cord of responsibility that ties us together. This is not being overprotective; it's how we are made: our children are never far from our thoughts.

And each new circumstance calls for a unique response. For example, when my daughter Adrianne had her first accident in my car, in which another young driver who was not paying attention hit her from behind, I asked, "Are you okay?" The car could be fixed. I was worried about how she was doing. After her second accident, in which she punched in the door of someone else's SUV, I again asked, "Are you okay?" But I also asked her how she caused the accident. While I was still concerned about her overall health and well-being, I was also concerned about her driving skills.

While being a dad has always stressed my improvisational skills, being a gay dad has truly been an adventure; I often say, "You can't make this stuff up!"

What I've learned is that when I was not "out of the closet," being a dad presented unique opportunities for growth and change on all our parts. But being a dad who is gay has added a dimension of complexity and thus has inspired creativity that I never had to call upon when I was playing the role of a heterosexual parent.

While there is no general list of rules to be the "best gay daddy in the world," some common aspects come in play as we raise our children—and they raise us. While the African proverb is correct—it does take a village to raise a child—so is this improvised proverb: it takes a child or children to raise a village, even when that village is a family. I am not only a parent because I have a child or children, but I am a better parent because of what the children in my life have taught me about the fine art of being a parent. Together—child, children, and parent(s)—we can make the future a better place for ourselves and thus for the coming generation of families.

Being a gay or lesbian parent means that we will constantly be in the "spotlight" because we are not the norm. We are the minority of the minorities. Although we are present in each and every religious community, ethnic heritage, nationality, disability-related community, and nation, gay and lesbian people are always a minority. Because of our minority status, some will find us "freaks" to be sought out and invited to parties because we are not like everyone else. We will be treated as if our "homogenous" grouping has a common voice.

And we are still under assault for being who we are by some in society. James Dobson is sure that our love is not the kind of love that makes a family.[4] Many homophobic people in the Christian church who are closet gays and lesbians will be most vociferous in their attacks on us and our families. The fight is constant. There is no "one last battle, and then we've won the war," to use an overly militaristic metaphor of other civil right movements. But we can make progress, although we will need to continually defend and, when necessary, speak out and offend others, so that our families will not be sidelined or marginalized, whether in church or in society at large. After all, there is nothing in Scripture, especially in the epistles of Paul, that says that we cannot be part of the body of Christ because we are gay or lesbian. In Galatians 3:28, Paul made it clear that in the body of Christ, because of our baptism, we are all welcome, regardless of the secondary divisions that separate us. In Christ, and thus in Christ's body, there is neither Jew nor Greek, slave nor master, women nor men, but only followers of the living Christ. Those of us who are Christians need constantly to remember that the gay and lesbian relationships we are part of and find great joy in are modern creations, and did not exist when any of the books of the Bible were passed down by word of mouth or written on parchment.

Here are some of the strategies that our families may employ when needing to be reminded of what we are about as we make our future together in a world that is changing:

- *Friendship:* As stated earlier, it is in friendships with others like and unlike ourselves that we learn the virtues as well as the vices of common life together. Whether the friendship is one in which we are overtly "using" or have a friendship out of great need, or is one in which there is a mutuality that sustains us, enabling us to live a good life, friendships of all kinds are important for the common good of a society.

  To this end, we who are gay or lesbian parents need to be active in being friends not only with other gay and lesbian parents, their children, and their extended families, but with others who may not be like us as well. Isolation, secluding ourselves in groups that are just like us, will not give us the opportunity to change the world. The way we will change the world is through rallies and parades, but not just through those festive celebrations; it is through the passage of laws, but we need more than legal fodder to change the world. Giving money to advocacy groups is a powerful tool but will not change minds, hearts, or attitudes. It is imperative that we work hard, if not harder, to be friends, using the persuasive power of love, with those who would alienate us, try to change us through force or reparative therapies, or outlaw our being full members of society. The key is relationships, one relationship at a time, which will inevitably change the world.

- *Alliances with other minorities:* As many people quote the World War II thinker Martin Niemoller, it is more true than not that many of our concerns and problems are ones that other "outside" minority groups face. Again, as Jack Rogers reminds us, the very words and tactics used against us to keep us powerless were used to justify slavery and oppress women before us.[5] As I wrote in the introduction to this book, the words that are currently used to deny us the right to marry are the very words, and thus logic, that was used in arguments against mixed racial marriages.

  It is imperative for us to side with and learn from others who are fighting similar battles with "majorities" in this country and to build alliances, because we, as a society as well as a church, are only as strong as our weakest relationships. We need to consider building alliance with African Americans, as well as with people whose ethnic and racial heritage is in Central and South America. We need to build alliances with people with disabilities and their respective advocacy groups, especially with those who are gays or lesbians in these groups, who are often treated as minorities within a minority when it comes to same-sex living arrangements in the community.

- *Playing:* It is important that we be seen on the playgrounds and playing fields, stages and performing art spaces of American society, as well as at amusement parks; as sponsors of NASCAR race cars; at the Kentucky Derby, Scottish Games, farmers' markets, parades, White House egg rolls, and memorial celebrations. Public exposure is only to our benefit. There is no doubt that the first time we come to a function in which there have never been gay or lesbian families, people may be, well, surprised (to say the least). But we can negotiate our way in and around the awkward social politics and make our case by simply being present, en masse, allowing ourselves and our families to be seen and known by others.

  For example, when gay- and lesbian-headed households decided to bring children to the Easter egg roll on the White House lawn during the Bush Administration, scores of reporters from mainstream media showed up to film the event. Bringing our children was novel, so we garnered publicity. The multicolored rainbow leis we wore identified us and our straight allies. My hunch? In the years to come, our presence will not draw the same attention because people will get used to our being there.

- *Listening and discerning: translators welcome:* We will have to be skillful in listening, really hearing and discerning, the needs and concerns of people as they voice objections or questions about our presence in certain activities in church and in society. As I said earlier in this book, we will always need to be ready to educate, translate, and make our points, our presence, known, time and again, as we move out of the closet and into mainstream American society. As I have heard the concerns of teachers and administrators, pastors and priests, civic leaders and family specialists, when asking (kindly) for our family to be welcome and included in programs and activities, I have had to put on the "hat" of an educator and explain, with little defensiveness, why we have a place in any and all parts of American society ... church included.

FEELING THE LOVE

At the end of the day, it is important to have a place where we can simply "feel the love" and be rejuvenated and refreshed. Always being "on" as the "gay parent" can become exhausting. There are times that I want to crawl back into the closet—not to hide because of homophobic slings and arrows, but because I am simply tired. We need to locate where and how we are fulfilled and feel most at home in order to do the work we do daily. After all, Jesus repeatedly withdrew from the disciples and the crowds in order to be alone with God in prayer. Not that any of us are Christ, but if Jesus needed a moment to breathe and recoup, don't we?

A BLESSING AND A CHARGE FOR LIVING LIFE
TO THE FULLEST AS A FAMILY

In conclusion, we are blessed by God to be parents and children, to be family with one another. God in Christ has, throughout time, continued to form and reform the Church universal, and is in the throes of doing it again. And God's Spirit is calling us to live truthfully, love fully, and be at peace.

As I tell my children, so I remind myself on this pilgrimage life as I follow Christ, the Pilgrim God: we are called to keep on living, one step at a time. Our future is always before us as well as in us, and is only brought out through the relationships we have with each other in life. If life is a pilgrimage, then we need to see, feel, hear, and sense the movement of the Spirit who calls us to live fully in the moment. To "be" wherever our feet are planted, at that moment, and to live fully in that moment, as gay or lesbian, bisexual or transgendered people, is the best gift we can give to ourselves, to our families, to the church, and to the world.

Acknowledgments

Never in my wildest dreams did I think that one day I would be writing this particular book. In my previous works, I tried to write in a way that would be literally, and progressively, all inclusive, and would stick in "people of different sexual orientation" when trying to list all who should be included in our practices as the Church. I did not contemplate writing a book that would include the entirety not only of my life, but the life of the visible *and invisible* Church. This book comes from a place that is closer to home, literally and figuratively, and came out of my own personal search for a book that was very close to my family situation of being a gay dad. I wrote this book with a sense of great excitement as well as with a tinge of fear, as both the publisher and I are taking a gamble. First, I was able to address an issue that concerns me greatly, teaching and learning what it means to be a dad who is gay in a Christian context. So there is excitement as I write this because I am living honestly, which was made possible by the Spirit of God who nudged, pushed, cajoled, and pulled me into the arena of living more authentically some years ago.

In the States, this is still a rather new phenomenon: stating publicly and openly that I am a dad who is gay as well as a Christian who leads and attends worship every Sunday. Many of my gay and lesbian friends still look at me on Saturday night, wishing me well as they plan to sleep in, read the *Times* or the *Post*, and drink coffee leisurely on Sunday morning. And for many the embers of faith still glow, but they no longer attend a congregation or parish for worship because they have been excluded by practices—of word or deed—that have made it very clear that "their kind," gays, lesbians, bisexuals, transgendered, and questioning (LGBTQ) people are not welcome to be "here," in a church somewhere, let alone participate in any part of the body of Christ. The great diaspora of LGBT from churches has been phenomenal in its sheer numbers, weakening the body by the loss of their fabulous array of gifts, services, and talents that made the body more vibrant and electric, with energy to love one another as God first loved and loves us. And the diaspora is not over.

That tinge of fear? I am an ordained minister of the Word and Sacrament in the Presbyterian Church (USA),[1] and we are currently not exactly open to ordaining gays and lesbians, much less marrying, celebrating, rejoicing, or shouting "Amen" when someone says he or she is gay *and* ordained, let alone in a committed, long-term relationship. And the U.S. Episcopal Church, which this publisher represents, is also facing the very same schismatic pressure as we are in the Presbyterian Church. While there are some who may look at this book as "fodder" for "defrocking" me, what these very same people cannot take away from me is the core reason behind this book: I am living honestly and openly, serving Christ, loving the next generation of Christians who are coming to take our place. If I am defrocked, it is my hope that the next generation, having seen the injustices of this age, will right the wrong perpetrated in the name of a god I do not know or want to be affiliated with, for it is not the God of Abraham and Sarah, or of Jesus or Mary.

But this book cannot wait to be written or published any longer. As one friend told me, a woman who waited for years until we began ordaining women as elders and ministers in the former United Presbyterian Church (USA), "sometimes we need to realize that the God who made this planet spin is not only going to work in the Church per se, but in the rest of the world too. And sometimes God is going to find more willing hearts, minds, and bodies to make important moves in the world than in the

Church, which is why God had so many more women moving to positions of power and authority in the *world* before it ever happened in the Church."

Being a dad who is gay is not a solo act: it is an act of many relationships, which I want to acknowledge. Those who taught me what it meant to be a dad are my children, Parker and Adrianne. In discussing writing this book with friends, colleagues, and the children, there was a lot of discussion about whether I should use the children's real names or pseudonyms. The children were almost shocked that I would consider not using their given names. Parker and Adrianne, this is your book!

I also want to thank both Dean my partner and Pam my former wife, who made my being a gay parent possible. Pam has been a terrific mom to Adrianne and Parker and has worked with me over the years to make sure that the needs and wants of the children are addressed above all else. Dean has been a great friend to the children and to me, providing them an ear to listen to their joys and concerns, a celebratory spirit for birthdays and graduations, and a steady stream of love.

To my parents, who taught me many of the "rules of the game" of basic parenting but who did not know until we were all much older that I was gay, thank you! I couldn't have written this book without you.

I'm also thankful for friends who encouraged me to write this book. After I had gone through the tenure battle at Duke Divinity School, Richard Rodriguez sat with me at a restaurant on the campus and suggested that it may be time for a book on gay parenting to come out written by someone with my background.

Paul Ilecki provided constant support and love during the first awkward days of my coming out, supporting me, my children, and my partner with great energy and true compassion.

Thanks also to the gay and lesbian parents and their children and grandchildren, whom I have met throughout the years. Glen with his daughters and son; Dan and Derrell with their sons Malik and Cameron; our former next-door neighbors Eleanor and Rhonda with their son Leo; Rich, Brent, Cheryl, and Abbie; David and Steven; Andy; Jay and Dominick; Rydell and his many children; Jeremy; Mark and his child; Philip in New Zealand; Erik; Shawn; Michael Adee (who is a fount of knowledge about LGBT resources); Katie, Paula, and Jordan; Deirdre and Julian; Charlie; John; Martin, who chased me out of my last closet; Stef; David and his daughter Fiona; Jamie from Australia and stories about his sons; Wally; Aelred, a.k.a., Rob; Andy; Rob; David; Eric; Jerry; Tim and Michael; Mel White and his family; David, Bob, and Elizabeth; David and Bobby, and all of their daughters and son; Dan Savage and his wildly hilarious and touching writings about his family; B. D. Wong's stories about "Foo"; Rosie, Kelly, and their children; Michael, Robert, and their children. And to all the gay fathers and lesbian mothers who talked with me confidentially and were living lives in the closet while I taught at Duke Divinity School, scared of being out, knowing that they would not be able to be ordained and serve the local parish. I hope that one day the light of God's incredible grace will break through the thin veneer of the closet doors, as it did for me, and you will be able to be more truly yourselves, wherever you are called to serve God in Christ. You have all been a source of stories and support, whether you knew I was listening and watching or not.

For those who have written on the subjects that I touch on in this book, I give you thanks. Your writings, speeches, and sermons have taught me well: Andrew Sullivan, Jack Rogers, William Stacey Johnson, the late John Boswell, Chris Glaser, Henri Nouwen, Dale Martin, William Countryman, Troy Perry, Keith Hartmann, Edmund White, Judy Shepherd, Paul Genet, Colm Toibin, Augusten Burroughs, Jonathan Rauch, Evan Wolfson—thank you for your bravery in writing books and essays that affect my life, and the lives of so many others you'll never know personally. If we meet in the near future, I'll buy you dinner and present you with a copy of this book, because I owe you a great deal of gratitude. You were all braver and happier than I was, once upon a time.

To Frank Tedeschi, editor extraordinaire, who took a gamble on me after I had been denied tenure at Duke Divinity School when few other religious publishing houses wanted to touch a faculty member denied tenure, let alone one who was gay,[2] thank you for believing in this book and in *Follow Me*. In the academic world of "publish or perish," while there were those who wanted me to literally and figuratively perish, you said "publish," and brought my words to life.

Thank you, dear reader, for listening, considering, and internally conversing with me about a life that I am still learning about, each and every day of the week, as a dad with great children who also happens to be gay. For those parents who are LGBT and are *not* out to themselves, family members, children, churches, spouses, or friends, all I can say is, Come on out! The water is fine! After all, God *knows* what is going on in our hearts. What is there left to hide?

Notes

INTRODUCTION

1. Frederick Buechner, *Whistling in the Dark* (New York: Harper & Row, 1988), 46.

2. The passages from Leviticus and Romans have been debated in other books, articles, sermons, papers, and presentations, and I am not going to reargue the biblical text criticisms in this book.

3. Even though Duke University has a nondiscrimination policy, because there is no state or federal law banning discrimination of LGBT people in cases of employment, Duke University could decide when and whether it wanted to implement the policy.

4. Robert Barret and Bryan Robinson, *Gay Fathers* (San Francisco: Jossey-Bass, 2000); and D. Merilee Clunis and G. Dorsey Green, *The Lesbian Parenting Book* (Seattle: Seal Press, 1995), to name but a few.

5. William Lederer and Donald Jackson, *Mirages of Marriage* (New York: W. W. Norton, 1994).

CHAPTER ONE

1. Margarethe Cammermeyer, "Foreword," in *Out of the Ordinary*, ed. Noelle Howe and Ellen Samuels (New York: St. Martin's, 2000), xiii.

2. Brett Webb-Mitchell, *Christly Gestures* (Grand Rapids: Eerdmans, 2003), 212–14.

3. John Westerhoff often refers to three types or parts of rituals or rites in community: rite of immersion into the community; rite of intensification in the middle of communal life; and rite of passage, moving from one community into another. The rite of passage best describes the coming-out movement or process of people who are secretly LGBT into public confirmation of who they are.

4. Never having been asked if I'm gay or not by a polling company, I am suspicious of the statistics.

5. Jane Levy Drucker, *Lesbian and Gay Families Speak Out* (New York: Perseus Books, 1998), 36–37.

6. However, there are small essays in some journals that focus on this process, such as Robert Barret and Bryan Robinson, *Gay Fathers*. Thanks to Richard Jasper and his website, Gaydads, for this reference.

7. Or "I'm a lesbian" or "I'm gay."

8. Sadly, some LGBT people have "come out" not by their own design or choice, but being outed by someone else. The politics of being outed are controversial in the LGBT community, and when someone, especially in public office, is outed, it is often because the public official brought harm upon other LGBT people.

9. Clunis and Green, *Lesbian Parenting Book*, 86.

CHAPTER TWO

1. Dan Savage, *The Kid: What Happened after My Boyfriend and I Decided to Get Pregnant* (New York: Plume, 1999), 204. He is quoting his child's inner voice.

2. From festivals.iloveindia.com, June 11, 2007.

3. The June 2007 edition of *GQ* includes an article entitled "A GQ Guide to Being a 21st Century Dad" with an image of Vernon Scott and Martin Lofsnes and their five-year-old son Demian Lofsnes-Scott.

4. Birthday cards are equally traumatic.

5. In an essay in *The Chapel Hill News*, Steven Petrow wrote that he and his partner go through the same thing, along with neighbors who stammer, "How is your roommate" or "your friend," and, even more broadly, "How is your ... luv-vah?" June 27, 2007, A7.

6. Drucker, *Lesbian and Gay Families Speak Out*, 37.

7. Ibid.

8. *Merriam-Webster's Collegiate Dictionary*, 10th ed. (Springfield, MA: Merriam Webster, 1993), 419. See also Random House's unabridged dictionary at www.dictionary.com; its definition of "family" also does not include specific genders or sexual orientation of family members.

9. The term "value" itself is an interesting term because it connotes something "of great worth," which is more of a commodity, an object, than something intangible and fluid like "love" or "respect." See "value" at www.dictionary.com.

10. Deirdre Good, *Jesus' Family Values* (New York: Seabury Press, 2006).

11. Rodney Clapp, *Families at the Crossroads* (Downer's Grove, IL: InterVarsity Press, 1993).

12. Good, *Jesus' Family Values*, 25.

13. I initially received this idea from conversations with Rodney Clapp, who put it in his book *Families at the Crossroads*.

CHAPTER THREE

1. Kevin Sessums, *Mississippi Sissy* (New York: St. Martin's Press, 2007), 286.

2. Report on CNN television, June 27, 2007.

3. In *Gay Marriage* (New York: Holt, 2004), Jonathan Rauch asks a similar question of a Kafka-esque world: imagine marriage has never occurred. No one would have a spouse; there would be no rules to regulate our relationships; no customs, rituals, or histories. Imagine an entire community without marriage (pp. 1, 2).

4. The national group is NARTH, National Association of Research and Therapy of Homosexuals, following the writings of Dr. Joseph Nicolosi.

5. Jack Rogers, *Jesus, the Bible, and Homosexuality* (Louisville, KY: Westminster/John Knox, 2006), 70. There are references and arguments about these passages in books by Dale Martin of Yale University and William Stacey Johnson of Princeton Seminary.

6. In versions like the New International Version, the word "homosexual" is part of the text, although it was not in the original Koine Greek.

7. William Stacey Johnson, *A Time to Embrace* (Grand Rapids, MI: Eerdmans, 2006), 18, 19.

8. Steve Hogan and Lee Hudson, *Completely Queer: the Gay and Lesbian Encyclopedia* (New York: Holt, 1998), 150–51.

9. Rogers, *Jesus, the Bible, and Homosexuality*, 17–29.

10. Andrew Sullivan, *Virtually Normal* (New York: Knopf, 1995), 13.

11. Good, *Jesus' Family Values*, 148.

CHAPTER FOUR

1. J. Anthony Lukas wrote a book entitled *Common Ground* that looked at the lives of three families in Boston during the first days of forced integration of public schools. It begs the question: What would happen if we intentionally integrated schools among LGBT and straight students, teachers, administrators, and staff?

2. Gigi Kaeser and Peggy Gillespie, "Arnaboldi Family," in *Love Makes a Family* (Amherst: University of Massachusetts Press, 1999).

3. While I am a product of the American public school system, my friends who went to either private Catholic parochial schools or to private schools, even those that mandated uniforms, still experienced being prompted to follow the cultural norms when it came to gender and sexual-preference roles and functions in school and modern society.

4. I understand that there are still high school proms that are segregated in parts of the southeastern parts of the United States, which reveals the kind of politics of segregation that continues in the twenty-first century.

5. LGBTS: Lesbian, Gay, Bisexual, Transgendered, Straight.

6. Kaeser and Gillespie, *Love Makes a Family*, 24, 25.

CHAPTER FIVE

1. Dan Savage, *The Commitments* (New York: Dutton, 2005), 41.

2. Drucker, *Lesbian and Gay Families Speak Out*, 36.

3. Jess Wells, ed., *Lesbians Raising Sons* (Los Angeles: Alyson Publishing Co., 1997), ix.

4. Urban Institute, 2007, www.urban.org.

5. Ibid.

6. Ibid.

7. Ibid.

8. Andrew Sullivan, *Virtually Normal* (New York: Knopf, 1995), 13.

9. Rauch, *Gay Marriage*, 3.

10. Brad Sears and Alan Hirsch, *Los Angeles Times* online, April 4, 2004.

11. Taylor Gandossy, CNN online, June 25, 2007.

12. *Newsweek* online, March 24, 2004. Because of this model of animal parenting, I have a tattoo of penguins on the right upper arm.

13. Kathy Belge, "Lesbianism in the Koala Bear," generationq.net, September 7, 2007.

14. Frederick Buechner, *Wishful Thinking* (New York: Harper & Row, 1973), 53.

15. Clunis and Geen, *Lesbian Parenting Book*, 148.

CHAPTER SIX

1. Andrew Sullivan, *Same Sex Marriage: Pro and Con* (New York: Vintage Books, 1997), xxi.

2. North Carolina is one, if not the only, state in the Southeast that does not have a constitutional amendment against gay or lesbian marriage. South Carolina, Georgia, Virginia, and Tennessee have added such constitutional amendments to their state constitutions.

3. Perhaps in Massachusetts, New Jersey, New Hampshire, Connecticut, or Canada, gay and lesbian couples honor their wedding date as recognized by the state or country.

4. Rauch, *Gay Marriage*, 3. As a gay man who was married and had two children from that married relationship, I am living proof that this equation is totally wrong.

5. It is important to note that Canada, and some countries in Europe like the Netherlands, had already passed laws recognizing same-sex marriages.

6. Rauch, *Gay Marriage*, 5.

7. Evan Wolfson, *Why Marriage Matters* (New York: Simon & Shuster, 2004), 1.

8. Ibid., 6.

9. Wolfson, *Why Marriage Matters*, 4.

10. Random House unabridged dictionary online, 2007. The word "marriage," which is either a derivation of the Latin word "man" or a Middle English derivation of the word "Mary," as in the Virgin Mary, is from the eleventh century. This is how recent the word and institution as we know it is.

11. Wolfson, *Why Marriage Matters*, 4.

12. I agree with Jonathan Rauch that "domestic same sex unions or civil unions" are merely ways to get to "marriage." See Rauch, *Gay Marriage*, 191.

13. Ibid., 67.

14. Ibid., 71.

15. Ibid., 23.

CHAPTER SEVEN

1. Jesse Green, *The Velveteen Father* (New York: Villard Books, 1999), 230.

CHAPTER EIGHT

1. Henri Nouwen, *Bread for the Journey* (San Francisco: HarperCollins, 1997), January 7.

2. Robert Fulghum, *All I Really Need to Know I Learned in Kindergarten* (New York: Ballantine Books, 2004).

3. From the *Boston Globe* online, June 14, 2007.

4. Much of this comes from Aristotle's *Nichomachean Ethics*.

5. Robert N. Bellah, Richard Madsen, William M. Sullivan, Ann Swidler, and Steven M. Tipton, *Habits of the Heart: Individualism and Commitment in American Life* (Berkeley: University of California Press, 1996).

CHAPTER NINE

1. William Stacy Johnson, *A Time for Embrace* (Grand Rapids: Eerdmans, 2006), 33.

2. Laura Benkov, *Reinventing the Family* (New York: Crown, 1994), 13.

3. Ibid.

4. See Drucker, *Lesbian and Gay Families Speak Out*, 20.

5. Wolfson, *Why Marriage Matters*, 4.

6. See Taylor Gandossy, "Gay Adoption: A New Take on the American Family," CNN online, June 25, 2007.

7. See Dan Savage, *The Kid* and *The Commitment.*

8. Clunis and Geen, *Lesbian Parenting Book*, 24–27.

9. Ibid., 171.

CHAPTER TEN

1. Brian Andreas, *Believing My Father*, painting, 1993.

2. Buechner, *Wishful Thinking*, 95.

3. Anne Lamott, *Operating Instructions* (New York: Anchor Books, 2005).

4. Taylor Gossandy, CNN online, June 25, 2007.

5. Rogers, *Jesus, the Bible, and Homosexuality*, 25, 29.

ACKNOWLEDGMENTS

1. I am fully aware of the years of amendments; reports; Peace, Unity, and Purity Task Force essays; the work of More Light Presbyterians; That All May Freely Serve; the Covenant Network; the Confessing Church; and New Wineskin Initiatives in my denomination. Ordaining those who are openly LGBT, as well as reaffirming the ordination of all those clergy who are LGBT but hiding in their closets, could not come soon enough for me or for the many others who are waiting for some hopeful action.

2. Some religious publishers refused to publish my books based on the secret yet widely known truth that I am gay. Being gay in their worldview is "moral turpitude."

Appendix

∽

FURTHER READING

BOOKS

While I have included some of these books in the endnotes, this is a collection of gay and lesbian parenting books that have been helpful over the years. This is not an exhaustive list by any measure, but a starting point for further exploring the literary resources in the world for gay and lesbian parents.

Benkov, Laura, *Reinventing the Family: The Emerging Story of Lesbian and Gay Parents* (New York: Crown Trade, 1994).

Clifford, Dennis, Frederick Hertz, and Emily Doskow, *A Legal Guide for Lesbian and Gay Couples* (New York: NOLO, 2004).

Clunis, D. Merilee, and Dorsey Green, *The Lesbian Parenting Book* (Seattle: Seal Press, 1995).

Downs, Alan, *The Velvet Rage* (Cambridge: Perseus Book Group, 2005).

Drucker, Jane Levy, *Lesbian and Gay Families Speak Out* (Cambridge: Perseus Book Group, 1998).

Garner, Abigail, *Families Like Mine* (New York: HarperCollins, 2004).

Green, Jesse, *The Velveteen Father* (New York: Doubleday, 1999).

Greenburg, Keith Elliot, *Zack's Story* (Minneapolis: Lerner, 1996).

Howey, Noelle, and Ellen Samuels, *Out of the Ordinary* (New York: St. Martins, 2000).

Johnson, Suzanne, and Elizabeth O'Connor, *For Lesbian Parents: Your Guide to Helping Your Family Grow Happy, Healthy, and Proud* (New York: Guilford Press, 2001).

Johnson, Suzanne, *The Gay Baby Boom: The Psychology of Gay Parenthood* (New York: New York University Press, 2002).

Kaeser, Gigi, and Peggy Gillespie, *Love Makes a Family* (Amherst: University of Massachusetts Press, 1999).

Lev, Arlene Istar, *The Complete Lesbian and Gay Parenting Guide* (Berkeley: Berkeley Tradeback, 2004).

Mallon, Gerald, *Gay Men Choosing Parenthood* (New York: Columbia Univ. Press, 2004).

Martin, April, *The Lesbian and Gay Parenting Handbook: Creating and Raising Our Families* (New York: Perennial, 1993).

McGarry, Kevin, *Fatherhood for Gay Men* (New York: Harrington Park Press, 2003).

McWhorter Sember, Brette, *Gay and Lesbian Parenting Choices: From Adopting or Using a Surrogate to Choosing the Perfect Father* (New York: Career Press, 2006).

Priwar, Shana, and Cynthia Phillips, *Gay Parenting: Complete Guide for Same Sex Families* (Far Hills, NJ: New Horizon Press, 2006).

Rauch, Jonathan, *Gay Marriage* (New York: Henry Holt and Co., 2004).

Savage, Dan, *The Kid: What Happened after My Boyfriend and I Decided to Go Get Pregnant* (New York: Dutton Books, 1999).

Savage, Dan, *The Commitment: Love, Sex, Marriage, and My Family* (New York: Dutton Books, 2005).

Snow, Judith, *How It Feels to Have a Gay or Lesbian Parent: A Book by Kids for Kids of All Ages* (New York: Harrington Park Press, 2004).

Strah, David, *Gay Dads: A Celebration of Fatherhood* (New York: Penguin, 2004).

Sullivan, Andrew, ed., *Same-Sex Marriage: Pro and Con; A Reader* (New York: Vintage, 1997).

Wolfson, Evan, *Why Marriage Matters: America, Equality, and Gay People's Right to Marry* (New York: Simon and Shuster, 2004).

Wong, B. D., *Following Foo* (New York: HarperCollins, 2004).

WEBSITES

Listed below are some websites and blog sites that are helpful in negotiating and moving forward in welcoming children into the lives of LGBT people. This list is not complete. Every day the list grows, with new blog sites and websites appearing every day. By looking at any one of these, a person can find links to other sites that might be helpful.

Affirm United (United Church of Canada)
www.affirmunited.ca

The American Fertility Association
www.theafa.org

Association of Welcoming and Affirming Baptists (American Baptist Churches and the Alliance of Baptists)
www.wabaptists.org

Children of Lesbians and Gays Everywhere (COLAGE)
www.colage.org

Dignity USA (Roman Catholic organization for LGBT community)
www.dignityusa.org

Disciples of Christ Church: Open and Affirming Ministry
www.gladalliance.org

Don't Amend.
www.dontamend.com

Family Pride Coalition
www.familypride.org/blog

Families Like Mine
www.familieslikemine.org

Freedom to Marry
www.freedomtomarry.org

Gay and Lesbian Acceptance (Community of Christ)
www.galaweb.org

Gay Family Foundation
www.gffonline.org

Gay Family Support
www.gayfamilysupport.com

Gay, Lesbian, and Straight Education Network (GLSEN)
www.glsen.org

Gay-Straight Alliance
www.gsanetwork.org

Human Rights Campaign
www.hrc.org/familynet

Integrity (U.S. Episcopal organization for LGBT community)
www.integrityusa.org

Lambda Legal
www.lambdalegal.org

Lutheran Lesbian and Gay Ministries
www.llgm.org

Metropolitan Community Church
www.mcchurch.org

Mombian (for Lesbian Moms)
www.mombian.com

More Light Presbyterians (Presbyterian Church [USA] organization for LGBT community)
www.mlp.org

National Gay Lesbian Task Force
www.ngltf.org

Open and Affirming Program United Church of Christ (Community resource for LGBT community)
www.ucc.org/lgbt/ona

Parents, Families and Friends of Lesbians and Gays
www.pflag.com

Partners Task Force for Gay and Lesbian Couples
www.buddybuddy.com

Reconciling in Christ (Evangelical Lutheran Church in America)
www.lcna.org

Reconciling Ministries Network (United Methodist Church)
www.rmnetwork.org

Room for All (Reformed Church in America)
www.roomforall.com

Soulforce
www.soulforce.org

Straight Spouse Support Network
www.ssnetwk.org

Supportive Congregation Network of the Brethren Mennonite Council for LGBT Interests (Brethren Mennonite)
www.bmclgbt.org

The Rainbow Babies
www.therainbowfamilies.com

TransFamily
www.transfamily.org

Transparentsy
www.transparentcy.org

CPSIA information can be obtained at www.ICGtesting.com
Printed in the USA
LVOW092018041011

249123LV00001B/131/P